P9-EDS-113

A Foreign Policy for the Left

A Foreign Policy for the Left

Michael Walzer

Yale UNIVERSITY PRESS

New Haven & London

Yale University Press books may be purchased in quantity for educational,
business, or promotional use. For information, please e-mail
sales.press@yale.edu (U.S. office) or sales@yaleup.co.uk (U.K. office).

Set in Janson Roman type by Integrated Publishing Solutions,
Grand Rapids, Michigan.
Printed in the United States of America.

Library of Congress Control Number: 2017942510
ISBN 978-0-300-22387-3 (hardcover : alk. paper)

A catalogue record for this book is available from the British Library.

This paper meets the requirements of ANSI/NISO Z39.48-1992
(Permanence of Paper).

10 9 8 7 6 5 4 3 2 1

For JBW

Contents

Contents

Preface

I wrote almost all of this book before the election of Donald Trump, and I made the final revisions in the first months of his administration and in the gloom of leftist expectation. What a Trump administration means for American foreign policy and for international politics is at this moment radically uncertain. But my readers won't, I trust, be living in a different world. The basic issues that men and women of the left need to confront will be the same. Who are our comrades abroad and how can we help them? How should we address the inequalities of international society? When should we oppose, and when should we support, the use of force? How should a mostly secular left address the religious revival?

I have been writing about these kinds of questions for a very long time. As a professor of political theory, I took advantage of the theorist's license to defend particular political positions in academic lectures and journals. But I wrote mostly in magazines like *Dissent*, the *New Republic*, and the *New York Review of Books* and sometimes in similar publications in Great Britain, France, and Italy. My subjects have ranged widely, but one recurrent focus of my articles and reviews has been on issues of foreign policy, especially the use of force by the United States, by other states, and by non-state organizations.

Seven of those articles form the basis of this book. I have extensively revised and expanded them, cut out (most of the) repetitions, and added citations and endnotes to pieces that originally appeared without them. Three of the articles were initially written for academic occasions and published in academic journals. But I think their style is only marginally different from that of the four others, which, along with the postscript, were published in *Dissent*.

My association with *Dissent* is now more than half a century old. The magazine—independent, left-wing, argumentative, and hostile to every version of authoritarianism—is my political home. I helped to edit it for several decades, and I have continued to write for it since retiring as co-editor in 2014. But none of my articles constitutes or reflects a *Dissent* "line." Members of the editorial board and others of our writers have always felt free to disagree.

Like all the *Dissent*niks, I try to write for the general reader, probably a mythical creature but at any rate not a professor. George Orwell's wonderful essay "Politics and the English Language" is our model: no jargon, no euphemism, no ideological newspeak. We aim at sentences that say, directly, simply, what they mean. I don't always measure up to that standard; none of us do. But I hope readers will recognize the commitment—which is also a commitment to democratic discourse, an engagement with our fellow citizens.

Over the years, I have been involved in many political debates, some of them fairly hot. Fierce polemics were a feature of the political world in which I grew up. The aim was to kill your opponent—with arguments, of course, not knives, but the arguments were meant to be lethal. In my old age, I try to argue more quietly, though I still believe that sharp disagreement is a sign of political seriousness. What engaged citizens think and say matters; we should aim to get it right and to defeat those who get it wrong. I understand the very limited impact of what I write, but I continue to believe that the stakes are high.

Many people have helped me think about politics and defend political positions. My political mentors (after my parents, who taught me never to cross a picket line and much more) were the men and women who founded *Dissent* and wrote for its early issues: Irving Howe, Lew Coser, Stanley and Simone Plastrik, Manny Geltman, Deborah Meier, Bernie Rosenberg, and Michael Harrington. My most active time at *Dissent* was spent with the next generation: Mitchell Cohen, Maxine Phillips, Mark Levinson, Nick Mills, Joanne Barkan, Jo-Ann Mort, Cynthia Epstein, Ann Snitow, Susie Linfield—and many others, to the third and fourth generations. These people are collectively responsible for all the arguments I make in this book, whether they agree or disagree. The magazine, now ably edited by Michael Kazin, continues to provide political space for arguments like mine and for important disagreements. Michael took time off from editing *Dissent* to read the manuscript of this book and make many useful, sometimes critical, suggestions, most of which I have accepted.

Among the writers who have had the greatest influence on my more recent political writing, two stand out: Paul Berman and Michael Bérubé. Berman preceded and guided me in responding to the religious revival and the appearance of Islamist zealotry. Bérubé has written a brilliant polemic against what he calls the "Manichean left" and has championed the work of non-Manichean leftists like Stuart Hall and Ellen Willis. I have followed in his tracks.

I have also learned a great deal from two very different sets of friends in Great Britain, the authors of the Euston and Kilburn Manifestos. Norman Geras, Alan Johnson, Shalom Lappin, and Nick Cohen are the Eustonites; Michael Rustin and Stuart Hall are the Kilburnites. Geras and Hall died very recently; they were briefly together at the *New Left Review*, breaking away for different but equally admirable reasons. I owe a great deal to each of them. But I am most indebted to Michael Rustin, with whom I have been talking about left politics for fifty years.

Finally, I want to acknowledge my friends on the Israeli left, who have had a major impact on my thinking—visible at many points in this book: Gur and Dalia Ofer, Brian Knei-paz and Bruria Shay-shon, the late Dan Horowitz, Janet Aviad, Gary Brenner, Avishai Margalit, Menachem Brinker (who died just as I was finishing this book), Yeri and Shoshana Yovel, Menachem and Nurit Yaari, Ilana Howe—old socialists all, like me.

Left politics is, as Irving Howe wrote, "steady work." I have a family of steady workers in all the causes of the left. Without their conversation, their support, and their love, I could not have written this or any other book. JBW is my steadiest, smartest, and most lovely comrade.

My editors at Yale University Press are not responsible for any of the political arguments in this book, but they are concerned that the arguments make sense and are written in decent English. I am especially indebted to Bill Frucht, who read one of my *Dissent* articles and told me that there was a book in embryo there. He has read and commented helpfully on every chapter. Once again, Mary Pasti has edited my pages and greatly improved my prose.

The introduction and chapter 1 derive from an article in *Dissent* (Spring 2014), 17–24, with the title "A Foreign Policy for the Left." Chapter 2 was first published in a festschrift for Norman Geras: *Thinking Towards Humanity: Themes from Norman Geras*, ed. Stephen de Wijze and Eve Garrard (Manchester: Manchester University Press, 2012), 15–26; my chapter here shares the title of my contribution there. Reprinted with the permission of Manchester University Press.

Chapter 3 first appeared in *Dissent* (Winter 2002), 29–37, as "The Argument about Humanitarian Intervention" and was included, in its original form, in Michael Walzer, *Thinking about Politics: Essays in Political Theory*, ed. David Miller (New Haven: Yale University Press, 2007), 237–250.

Chapter 4 first appeared in *Dissent*, Fall 2003, 27–31, with the same title as here.

Chapter 5 was originally the Spinozalens prize lecture given in The Hague as "Global and Local Justice" on April 7, 2008; a revised version was published in *Dissent* (Summer 2011), 42–48.

Chapter 6 was originally published as "Il governo mondiale e un sogno?" in *Quaderni Costituzionali: Revista Italiana di Dritto Costituzionale* XXXI, 1 (March 2011), 187–198. Reprinted with the permission of the publisher, Il Mulino.

Chapter 7 first appeared in *Dissent* (Winter 2015), 107–117, as "Islamism and the Left."

The postscript appeared in *Dissent* (Spring 2002), 19–23, with the same title as here.

I am grateful to the editors of *Dissent* for permission to republish (and revise) articles that originally appeared in that magazine.

A Foreign Policy for the Left

The Default Position

The men and women of the left—socialists, social-democrats, and left-leaning liberals, all of us—are most at home in the homeland; our politics is focused on the character of domestic society. Though we claim to be internationalists—and we are, some of the time— we have never gotten a good grip on foreign policy or on security policy. This is, I want to argue, a highly principled failure. We do best with global issues when they are most like domestic issues, as when we oppose inequality, sweated labor, and anti-union practices abroad or work across borders against environmental degradation. Our record is not so good when the issue is the possible use of force. That is something most of us don't want to think about—or we just want to say no. Bernie Sanders's Democratic primary campaign of 2016 provides a near-perfect illustration of this position, though not the only one.

Like it or not, however, we live together with our fellow citizens in an anarchic society of states where the ability to make wise decisions about the use of force is essential to the safety of our own state, of states with which we have close relations, and sometimes of people far away who are in desperate trouble and need our help. Wise decision-makers opt for peace whenever they can, but sometimes for a cold war, sometimes for the use of force short of war, sometimes for the threat of war, and sometimes for the agony of war itself. Political wisdom isn't essentially militarist or pacifist (or anything in between). It requires a steady commitment to conciliation and compromise so long as these are possible, and a readiness to fight when fighting is necessary. The two are equally required. That combination has always been a problem for the left.

There are leftists, to be sure, who are eager to support revolutionary wars, usually in distant places, and to endorse the violent acts, sometimes even the terrorism, of liberation movements. We are more hesitant when it comes to our own countries' wars, especially if we live in a great power like the United States. Then our standard argument is critical: anti-imperialist and anti-militarist. Over many years and many occasions, this negative argument is certain to be right some of the time. But when reiterated pretty much all the time, it amounts to a questionable demand for inwardness. Arguing against this imperial aggression or that military adventure, we regularly insist that our country should avoid all engagements abroad and devote its energy and resources to creating a more just society here at home.

Leftist conceptions of foreign policy, insofar as we think about foreign policy, lean toward the avoidance of forceful action. A commitment to neutrality in all international conflicts and civil wars is one example of this (think of social-democratic Sweden). Neutrality is a nice way of having and not having a foreign policy at the same time. But there are moments when it represents a critical and positive decision—as in 1917, when American socialists argued against joining the European war. The common man, John Reed claimed at the time, probably wrongly, "has a natural inclination to neutrality."[1]

Strong support for the United Nations and the International Criminal Court (ICC) is another example of leftist foreign policy. I remember how, after the 9/11 attacks, many American leftists wanted to turn to these institutions rather than act unilaterally or with close allies against Al Qaeda, even though we knew the United Nations and the ICC would not act at all. Perhaps that was the point.

A third, more curious but no less common example of leftism abroad is the claim that everything that goes wrong in the world is America's fault—and so we (Americans) should refrain from doing anything at all. The denial of agency to other countries suggests a fairly radical version of leftist inwardness; the lack of interest in what would happen if the United States actually disengaged suggests an even more radical version.

I will take up leftist arguments about revolutionary wars and liberationist violence, about the possibilities of global government, and about domestic (and foreign) anti-Americanism in the chapters that follow. Here I want to insist that the default position of the left, the position we keep coming back to, is an almost exclusive focus on how we and our fellow citizens live when we are among ourselves. For many of us, the only good foreign policy is a good domestic policy. Americans will be more safe in the world and the world will be better off, leftists have repeatedly argued, if we concentrate on creating a just society at home.

This is a very old position. It was first voiced by the Hebrew prophets who claimed that if the ancient Israelites honored the one true God by acting justly toward the men and women created in his image, if they stopped grinding the faces of the poor, he would protect them against Assyrian and Babylonian conquerors. They would live at peace in their land forever, and be a "light unto the nations" (Isaiah 42). All they had to do was sit still and shine.

> Thus saith the Lord of hosts, the God of Israel. . . . If ye thoroughly amend your ways and your doings; if ye thoroughly execute judgment between a man and his neighbors; if ye oppress not the stranger, the fatherless, and the widow, and shed not innocent blood . . . then will I cause you to dwell in this place . . . for ever and ever. (Jeremiah 7:3–7)

Act justly at home and your home will be secure—so says Jeremiah, and Isaiah says that people around the world will admire your light and imitate your justice. In the history of the modern left, it is easy to find activists and militants playing variations on these themes. I will offer just a few examples here; more will come in later chapters.

Consider Randolph Bourne's fierce critique of pro-war intellectuals in 1917. Bourne was "one of the strong and triumphant personalities" of Greenwich Village's "lyrical left" and also the most brilliant opponent of American engagement in the European war.[2] This is what he said about John Dewey, Walter Lippman, and other *New Republic* writers who supported the war: "Never having felt responsibility for labor wars and oppressed masses and excluded races at home, they had a large fund of idle emotional capital to invest in the oppressed nationalities and ravaged villages of Europe." This investment, Bourne insisted, was a mistake. So long as "the promise of American life is not yet achieved . . . there is nothing for us but stern and intensive cultivation of our garden."[3] He was probably right in his opposition to American engagement in the European war—though his reasons, I think, were not right. It is an odd leftist position that makes responsibility at home exclude responsibility abroad.

This argument has echoed over the years. Writing in the after-

4

math of the 2003 Iraq invasion, Andrew Bacevich, one of its leading opponents, quoted Bourne's line about "our garden" and argued that "if we live up to our professed ideals . . . we may yet become, in some small way, a model worthy of emulation"—which is to say, a light unto the nations.[4] I believe Bacevich was right about Iraq, but is a bad war sufficient reason for Americans to cultivate their garden —and do nothing more? In addition to Bourne, Bacevich also remembered and celebrated Charles Beard, the radical historian who was, in the lead-up to World War II, one of this country's most prominent isolationists. Writing in 1940, Beard defended "continental Americanism" and argued that America must concentrate its energy and intelligence on "overcoming the grave economic and social crisis at home."[5]

The default position of the left overlaps sometimes, as it did in 1940, with right-wing isolationism, but it is usually very different. Leftists, most of us, are internationalists in spirit even when we fail to be internationalist in policy. We know that we have comrades in foreign countries with whom we should stand in solidarity. Too often, however, we simply stand still; it is hard to figure out, or we don't try to figure out, what to do to help our comrades. But sometimes the spirit moves us in stronger ways—as when leftists from around the world rushed off to Spain to join the struggle against Franco and the fascists. That was a moment when the left actually had a foreign policy of its own—fight the fascists! The fight was organized and then betrayed by the Comintern, whose leaders were more eager to attack anarchists and Trotskyists than fascist soldiers. Still, this was a brief internationalist moment, when idealistic young leftists fought militarily in Spain while their friends fought politically in Britain, France, and the United States to end the embargo on arms for the Spanish Republic. How could democratic states be neutral, they asked, in a civil war between republicans and fascists? But only a few years later, after the Hitler-Stalin Pact, many leftists here at home were urging American neutrality in the war between Nazi Germany and democratic Britain. In an editorial published in April 1940, the now anti-war *New Republic* provided a perfect example of the default position: "It is not a mark of barren isolationism to believe with all one's heart that the best contribution Americans can make to the future of humanity is to fulfill democracy in the United States."[6] At that moment, the *New Republic* stood shoulder to shoulder with isolationist Charles Lindbergh and the America First movement.

The default position is sometimes said to follow from the uncertainties and ambiguities of international politics. Thus Jeff Faux in a debate (with me) about foreign policy: "Because the world is so complicated, the imperial reach so wide, and our access to information and our ability to process it so limited, the minimalist default position still makes the most moral and political sense."[7] Well, yes, it probably is a good idea, when you don't know what to do, not to do anything. In the years after 2011, President Obama was accused by neo-conservative interventionists of dithering over what to do in Syria. Given the complexities of the Syrian civil wars, dithering probably made sense. But a large portion of the American left wasn't dithering at all; it simply opposed any American action abroad, any exercise of American power. Leftists produced a long list of the disasters likely to follow from a large-scale US intervention—and then were hardly interested in the disasters that did follow when a very limited (and ineffective) American intervention was overwhelmed by the massive interventions of other states. Complexity wasn't the issue here, but rather a principled refusal to support an activist American policy in the Middle East, or anywhere else. Surprisingly, perhaps, most US leftists felt little need to stand in solidarity with the Syrian rebels, even those who called themselves secular democrats. Judging by our behavior, we were also only weakly committed to relief for the victims of the war—

and not committed at all if relief required the use of force (as the establishment of a safe zone in northern Syria would have done).

But later on, all of us supported the reception of Syrian refugees in the United States, and we were ready to take in far more than our government proposed. We argued forcefully against right-wing xenophobia. Once the refugees were here or on their way, solidarity was easier, for the issue now was the character of our own society. As leftists, we were proud to defend ethnic and religious diversity and to reject any curtailment of the rights of new Americans. And we were eager to argue that America, as an immigrant society, could be a light to other nations that had no history of immigration. We fell naturally into the default position.

No doubt, this narrow domestic focus makes a lot of sense. Randolph Bourne was right to say that oppressed workers and excluded races in the United States are our first responsibility. And we have a long way to go in the project that Richard Rorty called "achieving our country"—creating a fully inclusive and just society.[8] Though we haven't had many successes in recent years, this is where our voices are strongest and clearest. We stand in opposition to union-busting, racism, misogyny, xenophobia, growing income inequality, the role of money in elections and the advance of plutocracy, the pollution of the environment, homophobia, the attack on the welfare state, and all attempts to undermine the right to vote—I've put the list in random order because every group of leftists has its own priorities. But we all know the reach of leftist commitment, and we (mostly) support each other . . . when we are at home.

But that can't be the whole story of the left. So long as we are internationalists in spirit, we can't escape what Václav Havel, speaking to the Czech parliament in 1993, called "our co-responsibility for the cause of freedom and democracy."[9] In a world beset by wars and civil wars, religious zealotry, terrorist attacks, far right nationalism, tyrannical governments, gross inequalities, and widespread poverty and hunger, that cause requires intelligent leftist attention. Our deepest commitment is solidarity with people in trouble, and some of the worst troubles are being experienced, right now, in the world abroad. So we are going to be engaged again and again in arguments about how we can help people in faraway countries escape poverty and terror and how we can support those among them who are working for freedom and democracy. We will also have to argue about who, exactly, should provide that support, and when. This is a book about those arguments. It is an effort to answer the question What should the left's foreign policy look like?

The Argument Outlined

In the chapters that follow I have tried to join all the recent arguments about leftist engagements abroad. I want to address not only the state policies we should support or oppose but also the policies we should adopt, the actions we should pursue, on our own. We almost always think of foreign policy as state policy, and we certainly ought to take an interest in what our own state is doing in other people's countries (even if we think it shouldn't be doing anything). But the left needs its own foreign policy; we need to think about how our parties, unions, and nongovernmental organizations (NGOs) should act in the world. And since speech is action and words are weapons, we also need to think about what we ourselves say about international politics. We should write and argue in support of our friends and comrades in other countries and in opposition to the enemies of democracy and equality, wherever they are.

Since I mean to take a long view of leftist engagement, I will begin, in the first chapter, by describing some key historical moments when we got things right and when we got things wrong. In the second chapter, I will try to define left internationalism as it has been and as it should be—in order to explain why we need a foreign policy of our own and to suggest its necessary content. In the third chapter, I will focus, very concretely, on humanitarian intervention, a subject that has divided the left in fairly radical ways. I want to defend some interventions as legitimate projects but question the role of the United States as premier intervener. That will lead, in the fourth chapter, to a discussion of anti-imperialism as a foreign policy, with particular reference to America's hegemonic role in world politics.

In the fifth chapter, I will begin to address some global issues, starting with the radically unequal worldwide distribution of wealth and resources. What shape should the left's commitment to global justice take, and how does this compare with our more familiar commitment to domestic justice? The sixth chapter will deal with the desirability of a world government, which many leftists propose, often as an alternative to forceful action by individual or allied states. In the seventh chapter, I will look closely at the left's strange response (or non-response) to the global revival of religious zealotry.

In the eighth chapter, I will consider some of the reasons for our mistakes and failures and argue for a better leftist engagement with issues of foreign policy. Finally, I have added as a postscript a piece I wrote in 2001, immediately after the 9/11 attacks, which provoked a useful controversy and was the origin of this book.

What Left?

I had better say something about what or who I mean when I write about leftists. I began, in describing myself and my friends, by saying "socialists, social-democrats, and left-leaning liberals," but I want to be more inclusive than those words suggest. I want to include leftists with whom I disagree. Some people ask for singular or essentialist answers in determining identity: Are you now or have you ever been a member of the Communist Party? What does it mean to be black? Who is a Jew? Are you for us or against us?

By contrast, I am happy to give the question "Who is a leftist?" an open-ended response: Anyone self-described as a leftist is one. I mean to talk about all who claim the name. I certainly include the old left and the new, communists and anarchists, and all the people who have associated themselves with one or another of the popular fronts. Though I will write mostly about the American left, I will often wander into Europe, since the left begins there, and American leftists have often followed European movements. For a long time, the left's New York was a suburb of Moscow.

Pronouns are always a problem, and the plural pronoun "we" is the most problematic. I will use it sometimes to refer to my readers and myself, assuming that we are, for the moment, together. In dealing with American "imperialism," the pronoun links me with my fellow citizens; in writing about global justice, I use it to refer to all humanity. Mostly, however, I use "we" to encompass the larger left—since I am one of those who claims membership. Finally, there are times when "we" refers only to my section of the left, the democratic socialists gathered around the (little) magazine *Dissent* and our friends in the labor movement and in some of the left-leaning NGOs. I won't claim that this last "we" represents a major segment of the left, but I will argue that we *Dissent*niks have often gotten things right.

Readers should have no difficulty figuring out which "we" I mean at any time (occasionally I will add a parenthetical explanation). The last, lesser "we" will sometimes push other leftists into the category "them," but even though I will insist on contrasts and oppositions, I don't believe in absolute or eternal differences. There are important divisions within the left, especially on questions of foreign policy, but people do move back and forth across the lines. Solidarity and agreement are much more likely in domestic than in international society, but like any writer, I hope to convince all my readers and so produce a new leftist unity.

ONE

Moments in Time

Getting Things Right and Wrong

Some years ago, Richard Rorty argued that leftists should stop de-
bating their history and criticizing each other's past behavior. The
study of history should not be an attempt to figure out what happened, and why, and who was responsible; its purpose instead is "to
forge a moral identity" for the sake of our future politics. But surely
our moral identity depends a lot on what we have done, not only on
what we are about to do. "It seems shortsighted," Michael Bérubé
sensibly responded to Rorty, "to ask the left to stop trying to learn
lessons from its own past."[1] I mean to learn some lessons by looking
at key moments in the history of the left. Sometimes I will engage
in exactly the kind of criticism Rorty deplored, but there are also
men and women whose political work I want to celebrate.

What have been the characteristic views of the left about the
world abroad—when we aren't focused on politics at home? When
have leftists, rightly or wrongly, defended the use of force? The
recent arguments about what to do in Iraq and Syria led me to ask
these questions, but I am after more general answers. The ques-

tions aren't easy, first because there have been many lefts, and second because left views about foreign policy change far more often than left views about domestic society. Relative consistency is the mark of leftism at home; what I've called the default position is ever present. Here is a more recent example than those I discussed in the introduction, from the editor of an academic journal of political theory launching the February 2016 issue:

> I write as political attention in the United States and Europe is focused on terrorism. . . . Societies that are themselves wedded to violence—in the United States to gun culture, fracking, racialized killings, militarization of all sorts—express horror at forms of violence insistently presented as coming "from the outside."[2]

The clear meaning is that we should rather address the violence that comes from the inside. Indeed, there is much to address. But the outside also makes insistent demands, and it seems especially foolish not to talk about terrorism when it is on everyone's mind and where the record of leftist support or apology for terrorists abroad requires a strong critique.

But there have been many other deviations from the default position over the years, and it is with them that I want to begin; I will get to terrorism later on in this chapter and again in the next one.

Fighting for Socialism and Democracy

Enthusiastic support for revolutionary struggles in distant places was a feature of early American history. In the aftermath of our own revolution, Americans ardently supported the French Revolution (until the Terror) and the Greek struggle for independence. The Monroe Doctrine, announced in 1823, was a declaration of support for all the new nations of South America, "whose independence we have on great consideration and on just principles acknowledged." Prince Metternich of Austria claimed that the doctrine would give "new strength to the apostles of sedition and reanimate the courage of every conspirator."[3] Some American conspirators traveled abroad. Lord Byron had American company in Greece: Samuel Howe, "the Lafayette of the Greek Revolution," spent three years there as a military officer and surgeon. He later joined the Polish uprising of 1831 and subsequently had a long career as an educator and abolitionist in Massachusetts. In the 1850s, after the defeat of the European '48ers, "radical democrats" in the United States argued that when the revolutionary struggle in Hungary, Italy, and France "recommenced," as they were sure it would, Americans should support it, collectively and individually. "It follows from the history of French intervention in our revolution, that whenever the same occasion arises, we are bound to act a similar part," claimed a writer in the *Democratic Review*, the organ of the Young America movement. "The bearing of this country," Senator Stephen Douglas told the US Senate in 1851, "should be such as to demonstrate to all mankind that America sympathizes with the popular movement against despotism, whenever and wherever made."[4]

Nothing came of these fervent declarations (the revolutions didn't recommence). But this American argument reappeared in a more radically internationalist and militant version in the years after the Russian revolution. Now the default position was challenged by leftists who argued that there couldn't be "socialism in [just] one country." No left victory would be secure unless it was followed by many more. To be sure, the Bolsheviks weren't always sensible or prudent in their efforts to conjure up leftist warriors. At the Baku Conference of the Peoples of the East in 1919 (which John Reed attended but didn't live to write about), Gregory Zinoviev called for a "holy war" against Western capitalism. His largely Muslim audience responded with shouts of "Death to the infidels!"[5] Zinoviev's imprudent call has come back to haunt us (I will write about holy war and the left in chapter 7).

But it isn't only socialism that needs external support. Democracy, too, is a political formation that won't finally be "safe"—so American liberals as well as leftists have thought—until there are many more democracies. The effort to encourage communist or socialist revolutions abroad finds its parallel in the effort to promote democracy in countries where there may or may not be many democrats. These two together are the departures from the default position most likely to involve the use of force.

Consider the Red Army marching on Warsaw in 1919 to bring communism to Poland. That was Lenin's war; according to Isaac Deutscher, Leon Trotsky sensibly opposed it, preferring political rather than military support for foreign revolutionaries.[6] But since Trotsky led the army, he is commonly identified with the policy of forcibly exporting revolution. The American army marching on Baghdad to bring democracy to Iraq is another example of the same impulse. This war was supported by ex-Trotskyist Iraqi exiles (like Kanan Makiya), by European '68ers (like Adam Michnik and Bernard Kouchner), and by an odd mix of American leftists and neo-conservative intellectuals. The neo-cons can plausibly be described as Trotsky's political descendants, though they have forgotten entirely about socialism at home. Most European and American leftists opposed the Iraq war, an indication that they were engaged in a different left politics.

In the aftermath of World War II, there were significant American efforts to promote democracy abroad. Here, too, force is at least part of the story, since the democratization of occupied Germany and Japan are the key examples. Japan is the more interesting case, for there the writing of a democratic constitution was the work of American liberals and leftists (recruited, amazingly, by General Douglas MacArthur), who made a revolution in Japanese politics and society. The new constitution even included a clause about gender equality, which was not yet a major issue at home.

The Marshall Plan is another example of democracy promotion, although in this case in the interests of an anti-revolutionary or, better, anti-communist politics. Its key purpose was to strengthen the democracies of Western Europe against the perceived threat of a communist takeover. The plan was adopted by a Republican Congress, but it had strong support on what we might think of as the near left: the Congress of Industrial Organizations (CIO), after a fierce internal fight, and the newly formed Americans for Democratic Action. Irving Howe, one of the founding editors of the socialist magazine *Dissent*, writes in his autobiography that "only the most doctrinaire Marxists" could dismiss the Marshall Plan as an imperialist scheme.[7] But Henry Wallace and a host of American "progressives" insisted it was exactly that: democracy could be promoted only with the cooperation of the Soviet Union. The Marshall Plan, they argued, was designed to create American satellites in Western Europe. In fact, as George Lichtheim wrote in 1963 and Nicolaus Mills in 2010, the plan enhanced the independence of the countries it helped, even their independence from the United States—so it could plausibly be described as a leftist achievement even if it wasn't revolutionary.[8]

Support for revolutions abroad has not been a feature of American foreign policy since World War II. Some leftists, who probably don't know they are following in the footsteps of nineteenth-century radicals, have argued that the United States should be quick to provide assistance, including military assistance, to men and women fighting against tyrannical governments. But the more standard left position is simply that the United States should not help tyrants, as American administrations have done so often in Central and South America. As long ago as 1912, Victor Berger, one of the two Socialists elected to Congress, argued against an anti-revolutionary intervention in Mexico. I don't know whether he would have favored a pro-revolutionary intervention, but in 1916

Morris Hillquit (who was the Socialist candidate for mayor of New York City the following year) made the standard left position clear: "The people of Mexico will ultimately work out their own salvation if left alone."[9] There have been many such arguments since, which provide only passive support to opponents of tyranny abroad while leaving them to win or lose their own battles. They might prefer not to be left alone, at least not by their fellow leftists.

What if the left wins—as in Cuba in 1959? The United States had supported the Batista dictatorship but didn't intervene to save it. American leftists of all sorts urged the Eisenhower administration to seize the moment, join the revolution, and offer the Castro government political and economic support. Eisenhower dithered and then refused any assistance, choosing instead a policy of open hostility on behalf of American business interests. Fidel Castro and his friends, originally anti-communist, drifted leftward (that may not be the right directional description) as they became increasingly dependent on the Soviet Union. Castro described his capitulation in a statement that could have been read at the Moscow trials:

> At first the Communists distrusted me. . . . It was a justified distrust, an absolutely correct position, ideologically and politically. The Communists were right to be distrustful because we of the Sierra, leaders of the guerrillas, were still full of petty-bourgeois prejudices and defects, despite Marxist lectures. . . .

After that, what should American leftists have said? Certainly a blistering critique of US policy was necessary, but it was also necessary, it seems to me, to criticize the new Cuban regime.[10]

C. Wright Mills spent one month in Cuba (August 1960); he was taken around the country by regime-appointed guides, and he produced a book, *Listen, Yankee*, praising everything he saw, that became a best seller on the North American and Latin American left. Cuba, he wrote, was "a revolutionary dictatorship of the peasants and workers . . . legitimized by the enthusiastic support of an overwhelming majority of the people." ("I am a dictator with the people," Batista had claimed.) Mills didn't much like "the absolute power that this one man [Castro] possesses," but he blamed that on American policy (he wasn't entirely wrong) and refused to condemn the absolutism.[11] It's strange how the dictatorship of peasants and workers becomes the dictatorship of one man without losing its appeal. For years, with Mills's help, Castro had the enthusiastic support of the overwhelming majority of leftists around the world.

The Cuban revolution did have real achievements, especially in health care, education, and home construction. But at the time Mills wrote his book, two contemporary commentators reported that

> Fidel is now denouncing democracy as "old-fashioned electoral farces." People are arrested on suspicion . . . secret denunciations are encouraged. The jails have filled with political prisoners, and the government insists that people be "clear," that is, one hundred percent for everything it does.[12]

Few leftists in the early 1960s were willing to criticize all that—and US policy too.

What if the rebels lose, as in Hungary in 1956 and Czechoslovakia in 1968? I don't think any American or European leftists joined the right-wing demand for a forceful rollback of the Soviet empire. Indeed, it took some people on the left a long time to recognize tyranny in eastern Europe; the savage Soviet repression of Hungarian and Czech rebels had too many defenders. But 1956 was an important turning point for some leftists—and 1968 for many more. Unfortunately, many of those who turned away from communist tyranny embraced the newer tyrants of what was called the third world (Castro one of the first), forgetting what they should have learned from their earlier embrace. "When the glory of the Soviet Union faded," Leszek Kolakowski writes, "new lights appeared and at every stage we saw the same pattern: adore the despots and then escape and forget."[13]

Many leftists over many years defended Stalinist tyranny in the Soviet Union and in the satellite states—defended the purges, the phony trials, the labor camps, the transfer of populations, the mass murder of the kulaks, and much more—but did they actually adore the despots? Or were they "useful idiots," as veteran communists cynically referred to the naive, good-hearted men and women (often heroes of politics at home) who joined their front groups? I suspect there was both adoration and idiocy; it is hard to know which discredits the fellow-travelers more.

But there also were European and American leftists—these are the ones I want to celebrate—who denounced communist tyranny and supported the Eastern bloc dissidents, always in non-military ways. They helped get samizdat texts into print; they defended imprisoned writers and scholars; they rushed to Poland, Hungary, and Czechoslovakia to teach in the underground universities that the dissidents organized. This, too, is revolutionary politics, though it's rarely called that. The aim was regime change, and the changes that occurred after 1989 owe something to leftist help from outside.

The East European dissidents were a mixed bunch. They included right- and left-wing Catholics, secular nationalists, religious liberals, social-democrats, and people who dreamed of a reformed communism. Support for dissidence does not mean support for every dissident position. Politics is an art of distinction; I will be invoking this art again and again. It was (and is) especially important in the case of national liberation, a form of revolutionary struggle that deserves separate treatment.

National Liberation

The movements for national liberation that followed World War II were widely and strongly supported on the left, and the use of force by imperial powers was widely and strongly condemned by leftists everywhere. It is surprising to remember, but in the 1940s the Zionist struggle for a Jewish state in Palestine was enthusiastically endorsed by most American and even most European leftists. For example, W. E. B. Du Bois defended "young and forward-looking Jews bringing a new civilization to an old land." He always insisted, writes Harold Brackman, that the obligation of "the Negro people to support the fight for a free Israel" was closely linked to the obligation of Jews "to support the fight for a free Africa." Although the link wasn't yet established, Du Bois "was vociferous in his advocacy of the UN Partition Resolution of November, 1947"—as was virtually the entire American left.[14] This was the original "two-state solution." British imperialists and Trotskyists everywhere were, for different reasons, hostile to the idea. The imperialists thought national liberation was unnecessary; the natives were better off under British rule. The Trotskyists thought national liberation was a contradiction in terms: liberation required (and would have to wait for) an internationalist revolution.

But it was the Algerian war for independence that generated the most extensive and interesting debates, not only on the French left but also internationally. The struggle was led by the National Liberation Front (FLN), a secular left political movement whose militants had defeated other liberation movements, mostly by killing their members. The FLN's war was just, but it was fought in murderous ways that many French (and other) leftists defended— though these same people rightly condemned the murderous ways of the French oppressors. The oppressed, not for the first or last time, were awarded a right to be murderous.

Consider Jean-Paul Sartre's defense of FLN terrorism in his preface to Frantz Fanon's *The Wretched of the Earth:* "To shoot down a European is to kill two birds with one stone, to destroy an oppressor and the man he oppresses at the same time: there remains a dead man and a free man."[15] As I argued in *Just and Unjust Wars*, the claim that it takes one dead European to produce one free Algerian is ominous. There weren't enough Europeans in Algeria in the late 1950s to liberate the country by Sartrean means; more would have had to be brought over. Needless to say, Sartre himself did not volunteer to be the bird that gets killed so that the other can be set free. Arguments of this sort suggest a manipulative view of morality that is fairly common among right-wing "realists" but which clearly has its left-wing version. Why was it so difficult to support Algerian liberation and, at the same time, oppose FLN terrorism? I will argue in the next chapter that this is exactly the kind of politics that left internationalism requires.

Anti-Militarism/Anti-Imperialism

The defense of the use of force by revolutionaries abroad goes along with opposition to the use of force by one's own country. A wholesale rejection of militarism (and a reflexive refusal to vote for the military budget) is the most common left position. The pacifist left harbors a deep suspicion of every form of state violence, and almost all leftists are eager to support the peacemakers whenever peace is a real possibility (and sometimes when it isn't). Hence one standard argument, which is another version of the default position: only militarists and imperialists go to war in other people's countries. Leftist men and women understand that it is better to keep the "boys" (as all soldiers once were) at home. And if you can't keep them at home, then, as the Vietnam-era song has it: "Bring 'em back alive."[16]

William Appleman Williams, the Wisconsin historian who greatly influenced New Left attitudes toward foreign policy, argued that "the truly essential need is to re-examine our conception of saving other people and societies." The New Left, he wrote, should pursue a vision "based on self-containment and community."[17] Saving other people too often requires sending the boys abroad or, in more contemporary terms, putting boots on the ground.

In a great power like Great Britain in the late nineteenth and early twentieth centuries or the United States from the time of the war with Spain, anti-militarist politics is also anti-imperialist politics. The two go together since empires cannot be sustained without armies. This leftist blend of oppositions has produced some fine moments. One of my favorites is the appearance in 1898 of the Anti-Imperialist League, which campaigned against the American war in the Philippines (and also opposed US policies in Cuba and Puerto Rico). The league's members included Jane Addams, Ambrose Bierce, John Dewey, Samuel Gompers, Henry and William James, Carl Schurz, and Mark Twain, all of them arguing that democracy at home could not endure alongside empire abroad.[18] This might be another example of the default position, except that the American anti-imperialists were not interested only in democracy at home; many were also strong supporters of the Philippine insurgents. Twain and a number of others had initially supported the war against Spain—not an anti-militarist position—thinking it was a war of liberation, a revolutionary war. They turned against it only when they recognized the imperialist program of the American government. Now it was the Philippine insurgents who were fighting a war of liberation.

Mark Twain's pamphlet *To the Person Sitting in Darkness*, published in 1901 by the Anti-Imperialist League of New York, is a classic left text that ought to be reprinted every time anyone in the United States, or anywhere else, tries by force to bring the light of civilization, or democracy, or socialism to those who sit in darkness. Twain was more than willing to bring, not light, but liberty. The Philippine temptation was too strong, he wrote, and President McKinley had made a bad mistake: he played "the European game."

[But] this was the very time and place to play the American game. . . . Rich winnings were to be gathered in, too, rich and permanent, indestructible; a fortune transmissible forever to the children of the flag. Not land, not money, not dominion— no, something worth many times more than that dross . . . the spectacle of a nation of long harassed and persecuted slaves set free through our influence.

Let the Philippine people deal with their domestic questions in their own way, Twain wrote. "I am opposed to having the eagle put its talons on any other land." As the war dragged on and its cruelties multiplied, he wrote even more strongly. Here he is in 1906, after the Moro massacre:

General Wood was present and looking on. His order had been, "Kill or capture those savages." Apparently our little army considered that the "or" left them authorized to kill or capture according to taste, and that their taste had remained what it had been for eight years in our army out there—the taste of Christian butchers.[19]

Anti-imperialism also produced the campaign of British radicals against the Boer War, which approximately coincided with the American war in the Philippines. Mark Twain thought these wars were similar and required similar opposition. Indeed, we can find many parallel arguments by British and American anti-imperialists, but there was one significant difference. The British left in 1899 was viciously anti-Semitic, in the style that the German socialist August Bebel called "the socialism of fools." Leftists from the Social-Democratic Federation and the Independent Labour Party claimed that the war was the work of Jewish capitalists. "The Stock Exchange pulls the string and the British government dances," wrote the editor of a left newspaper. "But behind the Stock Exchange is the sinister figure of the financial Jew who is gradually enmeshing the world in the toils of the money-web which . . . the great racial free-masonry is spinning in every corner of the globe."[20] There were Jewish capitalists in America by the turn of the twentieth century, but they do not seem to have been blamed for America's imperial war. The Anti-Imperialist League is an example of principled leftist engagement with the outside world.

The same can be said for much of the left's opposition to US imperialism in Central and South America in the years since the Spanish-American War. US governments have strengthened the hands of local dictators who make deals with American businesses, and they have intervened, in both clandestine and overt ways, in countries where leftists have won elections or seemed about to win them. American support for the Pinochet putsch in Chile is the classic example, but far from the only one. The praiseworthy record of left opposition to all this makes it especially strange that many leftists, after arguing against every US claim to a sphere of influence in the Americas, hurried to defend Russian President Putin's claim to a similar sphere in eastern Europe. Surely left internationalists who favor self-determination for the people of Chile, Guatemala, and El Salvador should extend the favor to the people of Poland, Lithuania, and Ukraine. I will come back to this issue in chapter 4.

The American left's opposition to our entry into World War I is another exemplary moment, though in this case the left's weakness may have been the major reason for its excellence. While the large socialist and social-democratic parties in Europe, driven by the patriotism of their base, supported the war, the American party, with a much smaller (and partly new-immigrant) base, held firm to its anti-war position. What was going on in Europe, it maintained, was a struggle between imperial powers, unjust on both sides; the United States should stay out.[21] Bourne's "cultivate our garden" was the line also of many socialists. In a 1916 debate on the question "Must we arm?," Morris Hillquit concluded for the negative: "Let us center our ambition, our hope and aspiration on making our country the first great peace power in the world."[22] But American socialists were also internationalists who believed in promoting class solidarity across borders and hoped for revolutions abroad. I don't think they would have favored forceful assistance to those revolutions; they were all anti-militarists, opposed, like Hillquit, to preparing for war as well as to fighting it, but they would have favored political, diplomatic, and (if it were called for) economic support. So they supported the Russian revolution in 1917, but when the Bolsheviks established their dictatorship, many (not all) American socialists decided that internationalismn required political critique.

The early New Left opposition to the Vietnam War resembles the old left's opposition in 1917, but what followed all too quickly—enthusiastic endorsement of Vietcong politics—was neither principled nor useful. It is worth remembering that Students for a Democratic Society, which in 1965 organized the first major anti-war demonstration in Washington, DC, "insisted that there be no expressions of sympathy for the Viet Cong."[23] That was the right position, though it wasn't held for long. The revolutionary war was destined to end in dictatorship, the murder of thousands, the flight of the "boat people," and large-scale "re-education." By the 1960s and '70s, none of this could possibly have come as a surprise. What those years required was a hard, even paradoxical politics: opposing the American war and also its likely Vietnamese winner. Most leftists didn't like the paradox.

There were good reasons simply to oppose the war—much like the reasons for opposition in the Philippines and World War I. All of these wars, government officials told the world, were waged to save other people or bring them democracy (at great cost to their countries), and in every case the wars' opponents were right to refuse the mission.

But anti-militarism also produced one of the worst moments in left history—the opposition of many, though not all, British, French, and American leftists to rearmament against Nazi Germany in the 1930s. The argument for appeasement was mostly a right-wing argument, but many people on the left supported it because they were (or thought they were) anti-every-war. Clement Atlee, the leader of Britain's Labour Party, criticized the Munich Agreement in parliamentary debates; allowing Germany to annex parts of Czechoslovakia was, he rightly said, the betrayal of "a gallant, civilised, and democratic people." But since Atlee's party had opposed rearmament throughout the 1930s, he could not argue in 1938 for a war on behalf of the Czechs: Britain was grossly unprepared. On the Labour Party left, Sir Stafford Cripps opted for the pure default position, preferring a war against the British ruling class to a war against Nazi Germany. He thought the best defense against the Nazis was a socialist revolution at home. A minority of Labourites were committed pacifists, but most would have supported a war of national defense, as they later did. But they refused on principle to anticipate such a war or to prepare for it.[24]

Harold Laski, the Labour Party's leading intellectual, is an interesting exception. He was praised by the American leftist Max Lerner in 1940 as someone who "has had to do his thinking, as also his fighting, on two fronts—facing the enemy of fascism abroad and the enemy of capitalist privilege at home. It is a measure of his humanity that he knows which is the greater enemy."[25] Unfortunately, neither Laski nor Lerner fully grasped the need for another two-front war—against both capitalist privilege and Stalinism. Left internationalists frequently have to fight on two fronts—and sometimes a couple more (see chapter 8).

Norman Thomas and Bertram Wolfe's 1939 book, *Keep America*

Out of War, which called for a "reduction of the size of the military-naval budget," is a good example of the American left's position in the lead-up to World War II.[26] Of course, the American Communist Party favored whatever policy Stalin thought necessary to Soviet security. American communists were anti-fascist and in favor of rearmament in the 1930s until the Hitler-Stalin Pact brought a quick turn toward neutrality, America First, and the default position, which was followed immediately after the invasion of the Soviet Union in July 1941 by a fierce commitment to a war against Germany. Socialists like Thomas, however, were self-directed, and they chose pretty consistently to fight against the last war. "We were," Irving Howe wrote years later, "a war behind in our thinking."[27] Thomas repeated the arguments of Eugene Debs without noticing that Hitler's Germany was nothing like the kaiser's.

How could anyone fail to notice? The oppositional politics that leftists were most accustomed to, aimed always at American militarism (the country was in fact drastically disarmed in the 1930s), blinded many of them to the reality of Nazi militarism. Nor were they ready to acknowledge that fighting against militarism requires a military to do the fighting. Perhaps this is another example of the default position: only an America without an army could be a light unto the nations.

Leftist readiness to support disarmament and appeasement has another explanation: what I call the "politics of pretending"—which in 1938 and '39 took the form of insisting on the reasonableness of people who gave no sign of being reasonable. Paul Berman nicely describes the large numbers of French socialists who supported the Munich Agreement: "They gazed across the Rhine and simply refused to believe that millions of upstanding Germans had enlisted in a political movement whose animating principles were paranoid conspiracy theories [and] blood-curdling hatreds."[28] In the same spirit, later on, many leftists were eager to describe the Chinese communists as "agrarian reformers." More recently, many were quick to imagine Islamist zealotry as a (strange) form of resistance to Western imperialism. I am fairly sure that in each case, most of the people making these arguments knew, deep down, that they were pretending.

Just Wars

Opposition to the use of force is only a common left position, not a consistent one. Think of the International Brigades in the Spanish Civil War. Many leftists were ready to fight against fascism until the Hitler-Stalin Pact forced a large number of them into militant unreadiness. Soon enough, however, leftists recognized a more urgent and forceful militancy. World War II in western Europe was, in its leadership, a right-wing war, run by nationalists (and imperialists) like Winston Churchill and Charles de Gaulle, who had steadily opposed appeasement. Communists and popular front leftists were a major force in underground opposition to the Nazis, though (with a few exceptions) only after Germany invaded Russia. The default position had temporarily lost its appeal.

World War II brought one critical issue to the fore: many leftists, especially those influenced by Marxist doctrine, thought that once military force was justified, there were no moral ("bourgeois liberal") constraints on its use. But anarchists and pacifists, like Dwight Macdonald in his marvelous magazine, *Politics*, sharply criticized the bombing of German cities and the use of the atomic bomb against Japan.[29] Macdonald and his friends had opposed American participation in the war from the beginning, and they maintained their opposition even after they recognized that Nazism was not just one more imperialism. They got the war wrong, but they were right to condemn many incidents in the war's conduct.

On the other hand, those of us leftists who got the war right had little to say about attacks on enemy nations' civilian populations. Moral arguments would figure in an important way in leftist opposition to the Vietnam War, but they were rarely heard during the "good" war against Nazism and Japanese militarism—which invites a question: Are these arguments relevant to warfare generally, or are they merely useful in our anti-war campaigns? Macdonald applied morality consistently in World War II and afterward, but many leftists did not.

Leftists have supported the use of force—even by capitalist countries like the United States—in other instances. Some Marxist militants argue that any war fought by a capitalist country is, by definition, an imperialist war. But the war in Korea, which was fought by an alliance of capitalist countries, was supported by most people on the American and European near-left. A war against aggression, approved by the United Nations, could plausibly be called a just war. Nonetheless, there was left opposition: Michael Harrington, the future leader of Democratic Socialists of America, acting then as a member of the Catholic Worker movement, and David Dellinger, with the War Resisters League, marched against the war; I. F. Stone, bravely and (I think) wrongly, called it unjust.[30] The future editors of *Dissent* magazine, breaking with many of their fellow Trotskyists, supported the war, but critically, which was the right way to do it.

The US attack on Afghanistan in 2001 was another just war that nonetheless required sharp criticism. It was necessary then and in the years that followed to distinguish between the decision to fight and the conduct of the fighting. Ellen Willis did exactly that when she wrote in April 2002 that her objections were "from the beginning . . . not to the fact of our war in Afghanistan but to the way we've conducted it."[31] Since the Afghan war is commonly cited in leftist argument as a key instance of imperial aggression, I will take it up, and come back to Willis's commendable critique, in chapter 4.

In a history of the American left, Michael Kazin writes that ever since Woodrow Wilson's administration, "liberals had ardently promoted wars to preserve and advance democracy. The conflict over Vietnam put an end to that tradition for decades to come."[32] But by the 1990s, a more minimalist liberal and left defense of war had emerged—heralded by *The Black Book on Bosnia*, produced by the editors of the *New Republic* in 1996 and given full intellectual legitimacy by Samantha Power's *A Problem from Hell* in 2002.[33] The aim of humanitarian intervention was not to promote democracy but to stop mass murder, rape, and ethnic cleansing.

NATO's Kosovo war of 1999—driven in part by the Srebenica massacre of Bosnian Muslims by Bosnian Serbs—was a just war and also a near-left war: the Labour Party was in power in Britain, the Socialists in France, a coalition of Social Democrats and Greens in Germany, and the Democratic Left in Italy. The Clinton administration represented a weak version of this left politics, but it provided the leadership essential to the war effort. Military intervention in Kosovo was opposed by people on the farther left, who could not credit its humanitarian motive. I remember being told by a "refoundation" communist at the Gramsci Institute in Turin, Italy, in March 1999 that NATO "must be" aiming to seize control of the Black Sea from the Russians. There was no other explanation for the "imperialist" war. Actually, there were other explanations: some leftists thought the war was directed against Slobodan Milošević as the last standing Socialist, in an effort to complete the destruction of "Actually Existing Socialism" in the former Soviet bloc. Amazingly (since Serbia's "socialism" had little to do with socialism), a group of leftists formed the International Committee to Defend Slobodan Milosevic. Chaired by Michael Parenti, the author of *To Kill a Nation: The Attack on Yugoslavia* (2000), it included Harold Pinter and former US attorney general Ramsey Clark.

The more persuasive far-left critique came later: that left interventionism in Kosovo made the war in Iraq easier to plan and defend. But that can't be an argument against the use of force for urgent humanitarian reasons. It is instead (and again) an argument for making distinctions. The Iraq war was not a humanitarian intervention; indeed, it left the defense of humanitarianism in "tatters," as Michael Bérubé writes.[34] According to one of its justifications, the aim of the Iraq war was to overthrow a brutal dictator and promote democracy. There were left arguments and precedents for a war of that sort, but there was also a very strong left argument against it—an argument made, perhaps for the first time, by the US Socialist Party in 1917: "Democracy can never be imposed upon any country by a foreign power by force of arms."[35]

The Labour Party's David Miliband was right when he said in 2008 that during the previous decades "the neo-conservative movement seemed more certain about spreading democracy around the world" than the left did. The left, he argued, was "conflicted between the desirability of the goal and its qualms about the use of military means."[36] The qualms are reasonable when it comes to democracy promotion, but not when it comes to stopping a massacre. The campaign for intervention in Darfur, not the invasion of Iraq, was the closest continuation of the near-left's Kosovo war. I will come back to this issue in chapter 3.

Shortcuts

Arguments about the use of force for humanitarian or liberationist purposes are complicated; they require close attention to local circumstance and particular histories. We have to think hard about the relation of means to ends. Doing it right will produce judgments that seem radically inconsistent, though they are not: supporting Algerian independence but rejecting FLN terrorism, for instance, or urging American aid to revolutionary Cuba while condemning the growing authoritarianism of the Cuban regime, or opposing the Vietnam War while criticizing Vietcong politics. Ideological shortcuts, created to make the judgments easier, are popular among many leftists and require a left critique. I will just list the shortcuts here; much of this book will be devoted to criticizing them and arguing for a more reflective engagement with world politics.

The first shortcut is to pretend that oppression turns men and women into angels and to support the oppressed people of the world no matter what they do. But the oppressed are still frail human beings, and one of the reasons we oppose oppression is because of the pathologies it produces in (some of) its victims and the vicious politics that it (sometimes) promotes.

The second shortcut, perhaps more popular than the first, is to stand up always against "imperialism"—or, a shortcut inside the shortcut, always to oppose American policies abroad. Anti-Americanism is a common left politics, which, again, sometimes gets things right and sometimes doesn't. I believe that it got things right in Vietnam in 1967; it mostly got things right from the beginning to the end of the twentieth century in Central and South America; it got Iran right in 1953, when leftists criticized the anti-Mossadegh coup, and it got Iraq right in 2003. But that's not enough to make the shortcut a reliable one. The defeat of Nazism and Stalinism, the two most brutal political regimes in world history, was in significant ways American work. Many people on the left supported that work, as we should have.

In 1967, Dwight Macdonald wrote to Mary McCarthy that the American war in Vietnam proved "that despite all the good things about our internal political-social-cultural life, we have become an imperialist power, and one that, partly because of these domestic virtues, is a most inept one."[37] We are still inept: in December 2005, with 100,000 American soldiers in Iraq, we organized an election there—and our man came in third. This result may be without precedent in imperial history. (It might suggest that we were less interested in imperial control than in promoting democracy, though the Iraqi politician who came in first wasn't much of a democrat.) Macdonald's understanding of US imperialism reflects a political intelligence and a moral balance that are mostly missing in contemporary anti-American writing.

Another often used shortcut is to oppose everything Israel does and to blame it for much that it hasn't done, since it is the "lackey" of American imperialism or, alternatively, the dominant force shaping American foreign policy. The policies of recent Israeli governments require strong criticism—the occupation, the settlements, the refusal to suppress Jewish thugs and terrorists on the West Bank. But much of the left attack on Israel has little to do with its policies and more to do with its existence, which is taken to be the root cause of all evils in the Middle East. This view violates all the requirements of realism—by which I mean simply a readiness to see the world as it really is.

The last shortcut is to support every government that calls itself leftist or anti-imperialist and sets itself against American interests. This is different from the old Stalinist shortcut: support the Soviet Union, whatever it does, because it is the first proletarian dictatorship and the first workers' paradise. That kind of politics is, I think, definitively finished, though it had a brief afterlife focused on China and then, with very few believers, on Albania and North Korea. The more recent version celebrates Maximal Leaders like Gamal Nasser, Fidel Castro, or Hugo Chávez; there are also short-lived infatuations, such as Michel Foucault's affair with the future Ayatollah Khomeini. Leftist enthusiasm for populist dictatorships is one of our sad stories, which ends when resources run out, the failure to build the economy suddenly becomes undeniable, and the military takes over. But often the Maximal Leader is a military man himself, and the repressive role of the army simply becomes more

obvious over time. In Latin America today, the better left is represented by socialists and social-democrats in countries like Chile,
Brazil, and Costa Rica who reject demagogic populism and struggle
to produce economic growth, greater equality, and a stronger welfare state—and who attract less enthusiasm from American leftists
than they deserve.[38]

There is a lot to be said for the default position. We should work
in the place we know best to make things better. The improvement
of humanity begins at home. This argument has special force for
Americans, who live in an increasingly unequal society that is also
a near-hegemonic world power. We need to be wary of adventures
abroad that make our work at home more difficult.

Still, good leftists can't avoid internationalism. We will be engaged again and again in arguments about what we should do or
what we should urge the United States to do to help people in
trouble or comrades abroad. Sometimes there is nothing that the
United States can do, at least nothing it is likely to do right. But
even when we oppose American action in other countries, we can
be active ourselves—providing moral, political, and financial support to men and women fighting in self-defense or in defense of
others. There is no magic answer to the question, What should we
do? But the ideological shortcuts I've just described, lazily adopted
and rigidly held, have served us badly in the past and are almost
certain to serve us badly in the future. Sticking with them means
that we will get things right only by accident.

Political intelligence and moral sensitivity work much better
than ideology, and they are what should guide our choice of comrades and our decisions about when and how to act abroad. Dictators and terrorists are never our comrades. We should embrace

only those men and women who really believe in and practice democracy and equality. We should act abroad only with those who share our commitments and then, only in ways consistent with those commitments. This is the politics that I want to call left internationalism.

TWO

What Is Left Internationalism?

We all know what left internationalism used to mean: the unity of the "workers of the world," the solidarity of the working class across national boundaries. If we assume, as Karl Marx did, that workers have no country, internationalism is easy: the working class is already internationalist simply because it is the working class, exploited within a global capitalist system. And if the working class isn't internationalist, the problem must be "false consciousness"— the distortions produced by religious indoctrination, state education, and the capitalist media. Whenever the working class has its own agencies of cultural production, it will produce and reproduce proletarian internationalism. On this view, internationalism is, as we used to say, "the correct ideological position." It requires no political or moral defense, and since it reflects the actual interests of the world's workers, it is sure to be socialist in content.

But reality failed us here; the world turned out to be different from the way it was supposed to be. Workers did (and do) have countries, and they have very strong local loyalties that aren't plausibly described as false. False consciousness is not only a bad explanation for working class nationalism (and for the many instances of working class support for right-wing politicians like Margaret Thatcher, Ronald Reagan, and Donald Trump); it is also a pernicious explanation. Stuart Hall explains why the theory doesn't support a left politics:

> It is a highly unstable theory . . . which has to assume that vast numbers of ordinary people, mentally equipped in much the same way as you or I, can simply be . . . systematically duped into misrecognizing entirely where their real interests lie. Even less acceptable is the position that whereas "they"—the masses—are the dupes of history, "we"—the privileged—are somehow without a trace of illusion.[1]

And so "we" become the vanguard, claiming to rule the benighted "them" for their own well-being. This theory serves neither democracy nor equality.

I will come back later to the problem with all-knowing vanguards. Here I want to focus on the failures of standard Marxist theory and on the unexpected fact that the industrial workers of the world have been more loyal to their countrymen at home than to their fellow workers abroad. Marxists predicted that these mistaken loyalties would always make for a reactionary politics, and sometimes, certainly, they did and still do. But at other times they have proved invaluable to the left. Membership in a particular nation and the sense of solidarity with fellow members were key factors in the struggle for social-democracy and the welfare state. Strong welfarism is closely correlated with homogenous populations, and that correlation has produced opportunities for the left—and problems in broadly heterogeneous countries like the United States. But we have far greater problems when we move outside the world of fellow members into the world itself, for there is no automatic extension of loyalty beyond the nation-state, no group of people in international society to whom workers, or anyone else, have a pre-determined and necessary connection.

In the last four decades of the twentieth century, left internationalism acquired another meaning: not support for the workers but support for the victims of imperialism, the oppressed nations of the third world. It didn't seem likely that these nations would automatically produce a socialist politics, but the leaders of their national liberation movements often called themselves socialists, and they worked out ideologies that were imitative of Marxism even as they were also adapted to harsh local circumstances: undeveloped economies, undereducated populations, unreformed religions, and long-standing ethnic divisions. Perhaps inevitably, the adaptations went awry, and it soon became difficult to recognize any leftist content in third worldism. The new states produced by national liberation were often tyrannical, brutal, and corrupt. Some Western leftists worked very hard to love these states, but this was futile and ultimately dishonorable work. The states weren't worth loving. Today, from North Korea to Zimbabwe, they still aren't.

So a new shorthand politics is currently on offer: anti-Americanism. All we have to do to be good internationalists is to support the opponents of American hegemony. Among European leftists, an old maxim has been given new life: "The enemy of my enemy is my friend." Since America's recent enemies include Serbian and Iraqi dictators and its current enemies include radical Muslim jihadists, this is internationalism with gritted teeth. Happily, many leftists don't have the necessary grit. But anti-Americanism is nonetheless a popular politics in much of Europe, and if it doesn't reach to full support for every enemy of the Americans, it still reaches pretty far. It takes the form of apology and excuse or, more simply, a refusal to oppose America's opponents, however awful their politics. In the case of America's ally Israel, it goes much further. English leftists marching in London during the Gaza War of 2015, in support of Hamas—"We are all Hamas!"—certainly thought they were practicing a left internationalist politics. That Hamas was in no sense a leftist movement, that its militants were also religious zealots, made no difference, so long as it was hostile to Israel and America.

But the truth about Hamas should have made a difference. Internationalism is not the automatic support of the world's workers, or of every movement claiming to represent a colonized people, or of every opponent of the United States. It requires a more nuanced politics and a more open-ended search for allies. My aim in this chapter is to provide what might best be called a practical post-Marxist account of this search. Perhaps we need a new theory of internationalism, but what we need first is a close look at the circumstances in which we undertake "the choice of comrades" (the phrase comes from Ignazio Silone)—and at the political and moral judgments this choice requires.[2]

Our comrades are not given to us by the laws of history; we cannot identify them mechanically by their place in the class structure. At home, the necessary choices are relatively easy: most of the time, we find ourselves in ideological agreement with men and women who are already familiar to us, with whom we share a wide range of commitments. We come together without great difficulty. In the larger world, familiarity lapses, and none of the shorthand substitutes are much help: workers and peasants, oppressed nations, the victims of (American) imperialism. These are not men and women we know, and we don't easily come together with them. Many are passive and politically invisible—passivity and invisibility are, after all, among the standard effects of oppression. And when the oppressed are organized for political action, we see them only on our television screens, marching in demonstrations, shouting angry slogans about divine revenge or political destruction, invisible again in the crowd. How did they arrive at *those* slogans?

The people we actually encounter are militants who claim to act in the name of the oppressed; often they are members of a vanguard whose consciousness, they assure us, is true. It is the militants whose arguments we come to know—and they argue with one another as much as with anyone else. They hold different beliefs from one another, make different commitments. They adopt a wide range of ideologies and strategies—which are not determined by the global economy or the politics of imperial power, or else there would be no differences among them. In fact, the militants disagree in ways that are deep and often unbridgeable. Our comrades are the ones, and only the ones, with whom we share a politics and a morality, who reject vanguard arrogance, who aspire to rule with the oppressed, not over them.

But isn't left internationalism driven by a commitment to all oppressed people everywhere in the world—more than that, to people in trouble, whether or not the trouble is caused by recognizable forms of oppression? Yes, it is; the virtue of left internationalism is that it breaks with what Norman Geras calls the "contract of mutual indifference." We are never indifferent to the suffering of people in near or faraway countries. But when internationalists today reject indifference, it is not because we share material interests with the people we want to help or because we are acting out, with them, a world-historical script. As Geras argues in his meditation on the Holocaust, the only possible basis of the "duty to bring aid" is moral. "On its own, self-interest, even if this is the interest of a group, offers an improbable route towards a state of things in which sympathetic care and support for others will have come to occupy a . . . prominent place."[3]

This appeal to morality and sympathy profoundly revises leftist doctrine. If we are not moved morally, emotionally, by the suffering of others, we won't be moved to do what needs doing. "An ethic of mutual concern," Geras continues, "has to inform any worthwhile politics of justice, or equality, or socialism."[4] Yes; but the practical consequences of this ethic are not always easy to figure out. About whom should we be concerned? To whom, exactly, should we bring aid? Who will distribute the aid we bring to the people in greatest need? When is it right (or necessary) to use military force on behalf of people in desperate trouble? What political organizations should we support—and what forms of popular mobilization?

Unhappily, trouble and oppression do not guarantee political goodness, or even decency. They can breed their own pathologies, producing a politics of resentment and rage. And these feelings, which need to be engaged and argued with, are too often exploited by people who have no leftist commitments—or any commitments —that stand in the way of their own drive for power. The militants who act in the name of the oppressed are often the agents of a new oppression. Totalitarian movements, terrorist organizations, and parties with Maximal Leaders all claim to serve the interests of oppressed men and women, and all of them should be met with skepticism and hostility—skepticism because they almost certainly don't serve those interests, and hostility because they are, however they describe themselves, the enemies of freedom, democracy, and equality. Our comrades, by contrast, are the men and women who resist oppression and struggle to act justly while defending socialist or social-democratic values. Left internationalism reflects a wide-ranging sympathy, but it should also be a solidarity of leftists.

I don't mean to describe a sectarian politics. We can make alliances with all sorts of people, including centrist liberals and free-dom-loving conservatives. And we can—we had better!—live with the political disagreements endemic to the left. But there is a line that we should always be ready to defend, a moral line that separates us from all versions of totalizing, hierarchical, authoritarian, or terrorist politics.

Terrorism

Terrorism, we are commonly told, is the last resort of oppressed men and women (or of their militants); it is the politics of the weak. But terrorism is not a left politics—for three reasons. The first is that it is the work of the few, an elitist strategy that seeks victory without mass mobilization and therefore without a democratic prospect. This is the old Marxist argument against terror. As Trotsky wrote, terrorists "want to make the masses happy without asking their participation."[5] The second reason for opposing terrorism is that the decision to kill innocent people today strongly suggests a disposition to rule violently tomorrow. The third reason is that the decision to kill the "others"—Europeans in Algeria, Jews in Israel, infidels in New York, Sunni or Shi'ite Muslims in Iraq—randomly and in large numbers, signals a desire to destroy or subjugate the target population. In all these ways, terrorism reproduces oppression even as the terrorists pretend to be liberators. It might be possible to use terror and then get rid of the terrorists. I am told that within one year of Algerian independence, all the FLN militants who had been involved in the battle of Algiers were in prison, in exile, or dead. Still, the initial choice of terror and perhaps also the use of terror to deal with its agents are reliable indicators of the authoritarian and brutal politics that quickly followed in Algeria.

Left internationalists should never be defenders of authoritarianism and brutality. And yet some of us often are. Why? George Orwell provides the most likely answer: "I had reduced everything to the simple theory that the oppressed are always right and the oppressors are always wrong: a mistaken theory, but the natural result of being one of the oppressors yourself."[6] Orwell had served in the colonial civil service; most of us are not oppressors in that direct sense, but we are citizens of states that are engaged or complicit in some form of oppression—or have been engaged or complicit in the recent past. So our internationalism is often reduced to Orwell's simple theory. And the maxim that the oppressed are always right readily translates into the maxim that militants claiming to act for the oppressed are always right. That is not only a mistaken theory but, often, a kind of complicity in new oppressions.

Another reason why left internationalism sometimes leads to a betrayal of the oppressed is the belief of (some) leftist militants that our values have to be surrendered for the sake of historical advance. Freedom, equality, and democracy, they argue, are not suited to the brutal world of class struggle or national liberation; these values don't make for victory; they have to be sacrificed. Tenderhearted bourgeois liberals will never usher in the bright tomorrow. "We who wished to lay the foundations of kindness," Bertolt Brecht wrote, "could not ourselves be kind."[7] That is, we, living now, must be unkind and endure unkindness for the sake of those who will come after. But the surrender of leftist values at any time is a bad idea; its victims are not only squeamish liberals but ordinary men and women caught up against their will in brutal struggles. As the Jewish socialist Hayim Greenberg wrote long ago, we should never look upon any generation as an instrument to advance the welfare of another. "There are no transitional generations in history."[8] Certainly we should never consider ourselves transitional. A bright tomorrow in which we can't participate is not likely to be bright for anyone. "No Future without Us!" is a better internationalist slogan. On this point, Shakespeare's platitudinous Polonius was right: if we can't be faithful to ourselves, we will never keep faith with anyone else.

Facing Right

So left internationalists will have enemies on the left. This late in the day, that can't be a surprise. And yet, many leftists have not been as critical as they should be of third world tyrants and terrorists pretending to be liberators. Unhappily, it is still necessary to argue that left internationalism must always have a democratic and egalitarian content. The maxim "No enemies to the left!" is all too often an excuse for indifference to cruelty.

But once we affirm the democratic and egalitarian content of our politics, our major enemies are on the right, and they still have the familiar names: capitalism and imperialism. We oppose these two in our own country and in every other country, although the opposition is more complicated than it used to be—or than we used to think it was.

The first enemy of left internationalism is that other internationalism of capitalist wealth and power, unregulated or regulated only in the interests of the wealthy and powerful. The political economy of capitalism works to underwrite Geras's contract of mutual indifference.[9] Just as it encourages individuals to think only of their own bottom lines, so it encourages countries to aim only for their own competitive advantage. But if capitalism is morally corrosive, it is also an immensely productive force, which continues to have the liberating effects that Marx first described in the *Manifesto* and which helped create the modern world that we defend—but also need to transform. Capitalist corporations and their governmental servants will never by themselves address avoidable hunger and disease, work toward the elimination of global poverty, defend the environment, or accede to the empowerment of their workers. They must be challenged by social movements and subjected to the political control of a mobilized *demos*.

Left opposition to global capitalism is itself a modernizing force, one that seeks to turn the success of capitalist production to the benefit of ordinary people, who are commonly, in much of the world, people in trouble. As domestic capitalism was engaged and reformed by domestic social-democracy, we now need a global social-democracy to deal with global capitalism. We haven't yet found the political space for the necessary global organization, but we know our organizing goals: worker empowerment, democratic regulation, redistributive taxation, and welfare guarantees. Our comrades are the men and women, anywhere in the world, who share those goals, who work for socialism or social-democracy in their own countries and look, with us, for whatever space exists for international agitation and mobilization.

The socialist/social-democratic project also brings us into opposition to imperialism. I am going to criticize the theory of imperialism in chapter 4 of this book and suggest an alternative account —specifically of the American "empire." Imperialism as a materialist explanation of every policy, every act, and every war of every great power in world history too often misses the mark. But powerful states pursuing their own interests do try to shape the political or economic policies of other countries without regard for the well-being of those countries' inhabitants. This is an important story, even if it isn't the whole story. No one is building empires in the old sense of that word, but the exploitation of the weak is as common as it ever was. US engagement in Central America, Russian engagement in eastern Europe, and Chinese engagement in Tibet all provide useful recent examples.

Sometimes the troubles of weaker countries have deep-rooted local causes; not all politics is local, but some certainly is. And sometimes the engagement of imperial powers is actually beneficial. We are not root and branch opponents of American or European (or Chinese or Russian) engagement abroad. The US Marshall Plan of the late 1940s is an example of helpful engagement, which leftists should have supported, though many didn't; NATO's intervention in Kosovo is an even more interesting example of center-left parties' use of "imperial" power for good internationalist reasons. Global interactions are immensely complicated, and anti-imperialism should never be the knee-jerk politics it has become. Still, leftists should be fighting to change much of what the great powers and their economic agents do in the world, and we should be supporting great power opponents like the East European dissidents before 1989 or Central American, Middle Eastern, Chinese, or Korean democrats today.

What American policies and practices need to be changed?

- Political and military support for tyrannical, predatory, and corrupt regimes
- The refusal of transnational corporations, based here at home, to respect environmental and safety laws and to recognize independent unions when they operate abroad
- The use of force to secure strategic bases or establish friendly regimes, and the failure to use force to save human lives
- The gross inadequacy of resource transfers from rich to poor states and the unwillingness of the rich states, the United States first among them, to organize a global campaign to end poverty and control pandemic disease

That is a short agenda for left internationalists. I haven't said anything about the refugee crises in the Middle East, Africa, and Europe, where left solidarity is critically important, or about immigration policy in the United States, or global warming, or a war against terror in which we have enlisted the support of terrorist regimes—as we also did, remember, in the fight against Nazis and Stalinists. These aren't easy issues, and it is a great mistake to pretend they are.

Consider the key question about the international political and military alliances of our country: Which odd bedfellows are too odd or too awful to take to bed? There is no general answer; we have to look at each case, always asking which alliances provide the greatest benefits to the people in greatest need. In answering that question, we see American bedfellows that definitely don't meet the necessary standard (and some, given the alternatives, that do).

The NATO alliance is worth thinking about in this regard. Originally organized to oppose Soviet communism, it was condemned by leftists still struggling, against all the evidence, to defend that murderous regime. After the fall of communism, the NATO powers began a serious debate about extending the alliance into eastern Europe. Many leftists, along with right-wing "realists," opposed the extension; some of them, like Jeremy Corbyn, a future leader of the British Labour Party, called for their countries' withdrawal from NATO. It may have been right to oppose the extension or at least set limits to it; it was certainly right to oppose withdrawal. But what was entirely missing from the left side of the debate, most clearly in the politics of people like Corbyn, was any commitment to talk to east European leftists— Poles and Ukrainians, for example—and to consider the views or even the safety and welfare of the people with the most at stake. Surely left internationalists have to engage with our allies abroad before deciding whether to support or oppose our country's alliances.

This is an old story. The peace movement in Western Europe in the 1970s and '80s was watched with astonishment by dissidents in Eastern Europe, to whom the zealous peaceniks never talked. Václav Havel thought the peace movement was the "perfect vehicle for engaging, diverting, and neutralizing the western intelligentsia." (He thought this "with good reason," Tony Judt adds after quoting Havel: "As we have since learned, the British and West German peace movements . . . were thoroughly penetrated by Soviet and East German intelligence.")[10] What the dissidents needed instead, Havel argued, was a militant intelligentsia and an armed West defending human rights. He didn't want a war of liberation, but he expected ideological and diplomatic toughness. Leftists don't always have to endorse such expectations, but if we are internationalists, we can't be deaf to comrades abroad.

Consider now another hard question about leftist engagement:

Given the fact of global warming, how do we decide between our obligations to future generations (which may require us to slow down economic growth) and our obligations to the contemporary poor (whose well-being requires economic growth)? I suppose internationalists must also be intergenerationalists. Our commitment is to people in trouble right now and also to those who will be in trouble in times to come. To strike the balance between these two groups, we have to work through difficult arguments—with no help from the slogans of the old or new left. The communism of the East and the capitalism of the West have been equally guilty of environmental degradation. Future generations will no doubt include the workers of the world and the victims of global capitalism, but that isn't necessarily the most useful way of thinking about them. They will also include everybody's great-grandchildren—a new category in leftist discourse.

Striking the balance now requires us to prefer our great-grandchildren—to choose environmental protection over economic growth whenever these conflict. But this choice is much harder to make in poor countries than in rich ones, and the disparity has to be problematic for all of us on the left. Nor is it clear that democratically elected politicians in either poor or rich countries will act effectively to enforce the necessary choice. Environmental politics calls into question my argument about transitional generations. Perhaps there will have to be sacrifices now for the sake of generations to come. The global poor will rightly insist that these sacrifices be distributed justly, and we must support them—even as right-wing parties win elections in countries like the United States by denying that any sacrifices are necessary. Nothing is easy here.

An Internationalism of Agency

Faced with the scale of human misery in the world, left internationalism is first of all a politics of rescue and relief. Faced with the dangers of environmental degradation, it is a preventive politics. Faced with the organizing struggles of factory workers in countries like China or Bangladesh, it is an old-fashioned politics of solidarity. Faced with tyranny and repression, it is a politics of democratic agitation. It is not, either now or in the foreseeable future, a revolutionary politics. Except for a few sectarian Marxists, no one on the left expects a grand global transformation after which we will have no more troubles. But left internationalism can and should be transformative in addressing the crises of poverty, homelessness, predatory rule, ethnic cleansing, and massacre. Here, it isn't sufficient to relieve human suffering temporarily, in ways that guarantee the same crises will need to be addressed again and again. Our purpose must be not only relief but reconstruction: we want oppressed men and women to become political agents who control their own lives. That's why we support leftist parties and movements in other countries and defend the right to organize unions. Left internationalists help people so that they can help themselves. Recall Trotsky's line about terrorists who want to make people happy without their participation. We want to make them participants. They will have to make themselves happy.

An internationalism of agency: that is what the commitment to freedom, democracy, and equality means in practice. And in the world as we know it, the crucial agency of self-help is the state—I mean a decent state, in the hands of its own people. No other political agent can collect and distribute resources, provide welfare and education, regulate entrepreneurial activity, protect union organizers, enforce safety and environmental laws, and so on—the list is long. We still need global regulation by social-democratic versions of the International Monetary Fund and the World Trade Organization; we still need resource transfers to the poorest states (like those that were supposed to take place, and sometimes did, within the European Union). But the benefits of a redistributive internationalism will themselves have to be distributed by the recipient states, and if these states are not democratic and free, their citizens will never get a fair share.

Left internationalists once imagined that their politics would lead them beyond the nation-state. Maybe one day it will. But right now it leads us only beyond our own nation-state, to a concern with people from other nations who are not protected by a decent state, who have no means of self-help, who are the victims, endlessly, of natural disaster and human depredation. We are internationalists on their behalf; our comrades are those among them who aim to liberate themselves and one another. Those comrades may be workers, farmers, professional men and women, bourgeois intellectuals, or civil servants and bureaucrats. There are no class limits, but there are moral limits: our comrades are not Maximal Leaders, terrorists, or oligarchs. They must practice a politics of democratic solidarity with their own people before we can join them in a solidarity of left internationalists.

As I have just suggested, and as will become even more clear in chapter 6, my version of left internationalism is statist—because of the state's effectiveness as a political agent. But states are not the only agents; we leftists are agents also. We have to urge decent internationalist policies on our own governments, but we also have to learn how to help friends and comrades abroad who are working to reform or transform their societies. We have the means at hand, the established organizations of the left and the leftist civil servants who run them—labor unions, political parties, environmentalist groups, and the associations that defend human rights, political prisoners, and gender equality. An International Brigade of freedom fighters seems beyond our reach right now, but the activists who work for left and liberal NGOs like Human Rights Watch and Amnesty International—these are our international brigadiers. Later I will discuss the global civil society in which they work. Here

I want only to describe the role they can play in giving life to left internationalism.

Consider the case of Iranian dissidents during the past decades. They have risked a lot in the struggle against theocratic rule and for the most essential freedoms—of speech, press, and association. They have looked to the West for support and gotten much less than they asked for. When Shrin Ebadi, an Iranian human rights lawyer and Nobel Peace Prize Laureate, was speaking in London about her book *Iran Awakening*, she was instructed by an English anti-war activist not to denounce Iran's human rights record or even discuss it, because doing so would play into the hands of "warmongers."[11] This is another old story. East European dissidents were often criticized for strengthening the "cold warriors" of the West. People fleeing from communist repression were likewise blamed for somehow fueling the conflict, as Leszek Kolakowski reports: "The refugees from Czechoslovakia in 1968 were sometimes met in [West] Germany by very progressive and absolutely revolutionary leftists with placards saying: 'fascism will not pass.'" Ebadi responded sharply to the English activist, saying that "any antiwar movement that advocates silence in the face of tyranny, for whatever reason, can count her out."[12]

Ebadi is a firm opponent of Western military intervention in Iranian politics. What she wants is exactly what her critic withheld: solidarity. She wants "human rights defenders . . . university professors . . . international NGOs" to support her and her friends in Iran. It is important, she says, "to give aid to democratic institutions in despotic countries."[13] There you have a foreign policy for the left.

The same point was made even more clearly by the Iranian dissident Akbar Ganji:

> We don't want anything from governments. We are looking to the NGOs. And we want people to know what the Iranian real-

ity is. . . . The intellectuals, the media, and NGOs in the world have to draw attention to the human rights abuses in Iran. . . . I emphasize: we don't want intervention, we only want the moral support of the global community for our fight.[14]

Ganji is a liberal (the left magazine *Monthly Review* attacked him for being insufficiently anti-capitalist),[15] but in countries like Iran, liberalism is a radical creed. It gets you beaten up and jailed. Confronting tyrannical regimes, we left internationalists should also be good liberals.

But what exactly should we do? As with Eastern Europe before 1989, we should publish the dissidents' works, organize demonstrations and sign petitions against their imprisonment, write about and against the tyranny they experience, join them at meetings abroad and in their own countries, if we can get in. We should regularly ask them what further help they want or need. Do they want us, for example, to press our governments to organize boycotts of their country's economy? Economic boycotts are often painful for ordinary citizens, yet sometimes politically helpful; "smart sanctions" that deny military supplies to tyrannical governments are more likely to elicit support from comrades abroad.

International boycotts are most often organized and enforced by states; American and European sanctions against Iran in recent years are the obvious example. But this form of political action is also open to popular participation—as in the first recorded case, when Irish farm workers in 1880 refused to work for, and shopkeepers refused to trade with, Charles Boycott, the agent of an absentee landlord. Consumer boycotts have often been a successful form of domestic protest, and they have been tried, too, against tyrannical or brutal governments abroad. The test of their justice is the same as for any political action: Do they have the support of the people they are intended to help? And will they produce, if they are successful, greater freedom and greater equality for all the people they affect?

Academic boycotts of the sort currently being called for against Israel are a special case: special both in their subject—scholarship— and in their object, the Israeli state. Strangely, similar boycotts were never called for against the East European communist regimes, and there has been no effort so far to protest Islamist repression by boycotting Iranian universities. The arguments against academic boycotts are very strong. Universities are institutions whose excellence depends on the freedom that exists within them—so they are often relatively free even in authoritarian states, and they are genuinely free in liberal and democratic states. Because of that freedom, they are always centers of opposition to the government, as American universities were in the Vietnam years (anti-war militants in Europe never proposed a boycott) and as Warsaw University famously was after the repression of the Solidarity movement in 1991. More recently, in the Green uprising in Iran, students and teachers demonstrated in large numbers and with great courage. Despite the repression that followed, Iran's universities remain places where students study and discuss the work of Iranian dissidents and Western leftists. Similarly, Israeli academics have played a major role in all the organizations and movements opposing the occupation of the West Bank and other territories seized by Israel in the Six-Day War. Left internationalists should be visiting with and talking to these people, not boycotting them. Freedom of inquiry and communication should be the marks of the international academy, extended to every academic space. The left has both an interest in defending that freedom and an obligation to the men and women whose freedom it is, or should be. This also is internationalism in practice.

THREE

In Defense of Humanitarian Intervention

There is nothing new about disasters caused by human beings. We have always been, if not our own, certainly each other's worst enemies. From the Assyrians in ancient Israel and the Romans in Carthage to the Belgians in the Congo, the Turks in Armenia, and the Nazis across Europe, history is a bloody and barbaric tale. Still, the twentieth century was an age of innovation in the way barbarism was planned and organized—and, more recently, in the way it was publicized. I want to begin with the second of these innovations. It may be possible to kill people on a very large scale more efficiently than ever before, but thanks to the extraordinary efficiency and speed of modern communication, it is much harder to kill them in secret. In the contemporary world, very little happens at a distance, out of sight, or behind the scenes. The camera crews arrive faster than rigor mortis. We are instant spectators of every atrocity; we sit in our living rooms and see the murdered children, the desperate refugees. Horrific crimes are still committed in dark places, but most contemporary horrors are well lit. And so a question is posed that has never been posed with such immediacy or so inescapably: What is our responsibility?

This question seems to me particularly urgent for leftists, since we are committed (or so we claim) to solidarity with the victims of every barbarity. But humanitarian intervention in defense of those victims has divided the left. It has found support on the near left, as in the case of Kosovo, but frequent opposition on the farther left, which commonly denies the moral agency of great powers like the United States or the NATO alliance: these agents can't be moral. I joined this argument a long time ago on the side of forceful intervention in emergencies (and only then). That is the case I want to make here.

In the old days, humanitarian intervention was a lawyer's doctrine, a way of justifying a very limited set of exceptions to the principles of national sovereignty and territorial integrity.[1] It is a good doctrine because principles are never absolute: exceptions are always necessary. But today the exceptions have become less exceptional. The acts that "shock the conscience of humankind"—and, according to the nineteenth-century law books, justify humanitarian intervention—are probably no more frequent now than in the past, but they are more shocking because we are more intimately engaged with them. Cases multiply in the world and in the media: Somalia, Bosnia, Rwanda, East Timor, Liberia, Sierra Leone, Kosovo, Darfur, and Syria in the recent past. The last three of these have dominated political debates on the left—along with Iraq, a false case, since the war there was never a humanitarian intervention; the claim that it was has made all interventionist arguments more difficult. But I want to step back from these recent cases, reach for a wider range of examples, and try to answer four questions about humanitarian intervention: What are its occasions? Who are its preferred agents? How should the agents act to meet the occasions? and When is it time to end the intervention? In answering these questions, I will address the key leftist objections to the interventionist enterprise.

Occasions

The occasions have to be extreme if they are to justify the use of force across an international boundary. Not every human rights violation is a justification. The common brutalities of authoritarian politics, the daily oppressiveness of traditional social practices—these have to be dealt with locally, by the people who know the politics and who resist the practices. Leftists (liberals, too) can help from the outside by providing political support and encouragement, by publicizing the brutalities (as Human Rights Watch does), and by welcoming exiled dissidents. But the failure of the people on the inside, with whatever help, to quickly reduce the incidence of brutality and oppression isn't a sufficient reason for foreigners to invade their country. Foreign politicians and soldiers are too likely to misread the situation, to underestimate the force required to change it, or to stimulate a nationalist or patriotic reaction in defense of the brutal politics and oppressive practices. Social change is best achieved from within.

I want to insist on this point. I don't mean to describe a continuum that begins with common nastiness and ends with genocide but rather a sharp break, a chasm, with nastiness on one side and genocide on the other. We should not allow ourselves to approach genocide by degrees. On this side of the chasm, we can mark out a continuum of brutality and oppression, and somewhere along this continuum we (left internationalists) should begin to work with the internal opponents of brutality and oppression, aiming at an international response short of military force. Diplomatic pressure and economic sanctions (smart sanctions, directed at the government, not the people) imposed by some ad hoc coalition of interested states: these are useful ways of engaging tyrannical regimes. Or perhaps we should aim at a more established regional or global authority that could regulate the imposition of sanctions, carefully matching their severity to the severity of the oppression. But these are still external acts; they are efforts to prompt but not preempt an internal response. They still assume the value, and hold open the possibility, of domestic politics. The engaged states or the regional or global authorities bring pressure to bear on the country from the outside and wait for something to happen inside.

But on the far side of the chasm, when what is going on is the ethnic cleansing of a province or country or the systematic massacre of a religious or national community, it seems foolish to wait for a local response. The stakes are too high, the suffering already too great; and the people directly at risk may have no capacity to respond, their fellow citizens no will to respond. The victims are weak and vulnerable; their enemies are cruel; their neighbors indifferent or frightened. The rest of us watch and are shocked. This is the occasion for intervention, and people who live on the left should be the first to recognize the occasion and sound the alarm. But intervention is not just a left project. When 191 member states of the UN General Assembly voted for the "Responsibility to Protect" (R2P), they recognized that intervention against "genocide [and] massive human rights abuses" is a universal project. Humanitarian intervention is humanity's work (I will argue in chapter 5 that global justice is, too).

Here is the limit of state sovereignty: since states exist first of all to defend the physical safety of their citizens, they forfeit their sovereign rights whenever they fail in that task—when they themselves attack their citizens or when they can no longer guarantee their citizens' security against marauding warlords or murderous religious sects. That is when external force is justified or perhaps required. "Defending human beings," Václav Havel wrote in defense of the Kosovo intervention, "is a higher responsibility than respecting the inviolability of a state."[2]

We will need to argue about each occasion for humanitarian intervention, but the list I provided earlier seems fairly obvious. (In the case of Syria, there were many calls for political as well as humanitarian intervention. I am writing here only about the second of these: help was urgently needed, desperately asked for, and not—as of this moment—provided.) The intervening army, these days, will claim to be protecting human rights, and that would have been a plausible and fully comprehensible claim in each of the cases on my list. We are best served by a stark and minimalist understanding of the human rights that justify intervention: it is life and liberty that are at stake. With regard to these two, the language of rights is readily available and sufficiently understood across the globe. Still, we could as easily say that what is being enforced, and what should be enforced, is simple decency.

Even with this minimalist understanding of human rights, even with a commitment to nothing more than decency, there are more occasions for intervention than there are actual interventions. When the oppressors are too powerful, even the most shocking oppression is rarely challenged. This obvious truth is often used as an argument against the interventions that do take place. It is hypocritical, critics say to the humanitarian politicians or soldiers, to intervene in this case when you didn't intervene in that one, as if, having declined to challenge China in Tibet, the United Nations—more specifically, the Australians—should have stayed out of East Timor for the sake of moral consistency. This is the criticism that I have heard most often as I have traveled and talked about humanitarian intervention over the past decades. But consistency is not the issue. We (the advocates of intervention and the intervening states) can't meet all our occasions; we rightly calculate the risks in each one. We need to ask what the costs of intervention will be for the people being rescued, for the rescuers, and for everyone else. And then we can only do . . . what we can do.

The standard cases have a standard form: a government, an army, a police force, tyrannically controlled, attacks its own people or some subset of its own people—a vulnerable minority, say, territorially based or dispersed throughout the country. The attack takes place within the country's borders; it doesn't require any boundary crossings; it is an exercise of sovereign power. There is no invading army to resist and beat back. Instead, the rescuing forces are themselves the invaders; they are the ones who, in the strict sense of international law, begin the war. But they come into a situation where the moral stakes are clear: the state agents of oppression are readily identifiable; their victims are plain to see; the war is just.

Even in the list with which I started, however, there are nonstandard cases—Sierra Leone is the clearest example—where the state apparatus isn't the villain, and the administration of brutality is decentralized, anarchic, almost random. It isn't the power of the oppressors that interventionists have to worry about but the amorphousness of the oppression. I won't have much to say about cases like this. Intervention is clearly justified but, right now at least, it's unclear how it should be undertaken. Perhaps there is not much to do beyond what the British did in Sierra Leone in 2000: they fought the rebel militias, strengthened the army, enabled a ceasefire, and reduced the scope of the killings.

Agents
We can only do . . . what we can do: who is this "we"? The Kosovo debate focused on the United States, NATO, and the United Nations as agents of military intervention.[3] These are indeed three political collectives capable of agency, but by no means the only three. The United States and NATO generate suspicion on some

parts of the left because of their readiness to act unilaterally and their presumed imperial ambitions (the presumption isn't crazy, but it also isn't, as some leftists believe, always right). The United Nations generates skepticism among right-wingers, but also among tough-minded leftists, because of its political weakness and military ineffectiveness. We are more likely to understand the problems of agency if we start with other agents. The most successful interventions in the past half-century have been acts of war by neighboring states: Vietnam in Cambodia, India in East Pakistan (now Bangladesh), Tanzania (twice) in Uganda, Australia in East Timor. These are useful examples for testing arguments about intervention because they don't involve the great powers; they don't require us to consult a theory of imperialism, Lenin's or any other. In each case there were horrifying acts that should have been stopped, and agents who more or less succeeded in stopping them. So let's use these cases to address the two questions about agency most commonly posed by leftist critics of intervention: First, does it matter that the agents acted alone, without UN authorization? They enacted the R2P doctrine before it was officially proclaimed. Second, does it matter that their motives were not wholly (or even chiefly) altruistic?

In the history of humanitarian intervention, unilateralism is far more common than its opposite. One reason is obvious: the great reluctance of most states to cede the leadership of their armed forces to an organization they don't control. But unilateralism may also follow from the need for an immediate response to an act that shocks the collective conscience. Imagine a case where the shock doesn't have anything to do with human evildoing: a fire in a neighbor's house in a new town where there is no fire department. It wouldn't make much sense to call a meeting of the block association while the house is burning and vote on whether to help. It would make even less sense to give a veto on helping to the three richest families on the block. I don't think that the case would be all that different if, instead of a fire, there was a brutal husband, no police department, and screams for help in the night. Here, too, the block association is of little use; neighborly unilateralism seems entirely justified. Anyone who can help should help. That sounds like a plausible maxim for humanitarian intervention: whoever can, should.

Now let's imagine a block association or an international organization that planned responses in advance, that prepared for the fire, or the scream in the night, or the mass murder. Certain people or specially recruited military forces would be delegated to act in a crisis, and the definition of a crisis would be determined—as best it can be—in advance, in exactly the kind of meeting that seems so implausible and morally inappropriate when immediate action is necessary. Even with planned responses the political or military commanders of an army marching across an international frontier, like the person who rushes into a neighbor's house when screams are heard, would have to act on their own understanding of the unfolding events and on their own interpretation of the responsibility they have been given. But now they act under specified constraints, and they can call on the help of those in whose name they are acting. This is the form that multilateral intervention is most likely to take if the United Nations, say, were ever to authorize it in advance of a particular crisis. It seems preferable to the different unilateral alternatives, since it involves some prior warning, an agreed-upon description of the occasions for intervention, and the prospect of overwhelming force.

But is it preferable right now, given the inadequacies of the United Nations? When police forces are effective in domestic society, what makes them so is their commitment to the entire body of citizens from which they are drawn and the citizens' (relative) trust in that commitment. But the UN General Assembly and Security Council, so far, give little evidence of being so committed, and there can't be many people in the world today who would willingly entrust their lives to UN police. In any of my examples, if the authorized agents of the United Nations or their domestic equivalents decided not to intervene while the fire was still burning, or the screams could still be heard, or the murders continued—then unilateralist rights and obligations would be instantly restored. Collective decisions to act may exclude unilateral action, but collective decisions not to act do not have the same effect. In this sense, unilateralism is the necessary fallback response when the common conscience is shocked. If there is no collective response, anyone can respond. If no one is acting, someone should.

In the cases of Cambodia, East Pakistan, and Uganda, there were no prior arrangements and no authorized agents. Had the UN Security Council or General Assembly been called into session, it would almost certainly have decided against intervention, probably by majority vote and, in any case, because of a great power veto. Anyone acting to shut down the Khmer Rouge killing fields, to stem the tide of Bengalese refugees, or to stop Idi Amin's butchery would have had to act unilaterally. Everything depended on the political decision of a single state.

Do singular agents have a right to act? Or do they have an obligation to act? I have been using both words, but they don't always go together: there can be rights without obligations. In Good Samaritan cases in domestic society, we commonly say that passersby are (morally if not legally) bound to respond to the injured stranger by the side of the road or to the cry of a child drowning in the lake. They are not, however, bound to risk their lives.[4] If giving assistance entails such a risk, they have a right to respond; responding is certainly a good thing and possibly the right thing to do; but they are not morally bound to do it.

But military interventions across international boundaries always impose risks on the intervening forces. So perhaps there is no obligation here either; perhaps there is a right to intervene but also a right to refuse the risks, to maintain a kind of neutrality—even between murderers and their victims. Leftist citizens should urge their country to intervene, but in the end, intervention is optional. Perhaps military action in such a case is an example of what philosophers call an "imperfect" duty: someone should stop the awfulness, but it isn't possible to give that someone a name, to point a finger, say, at a particular country. The problem of imperfect duty yields best to multilateral solutions: we assign responsibility in advance through some commonly accepted decision procedure.

But perhaps, again, these descriptions are too weak. I am inclined to say that intervention is more than a right and more than an imperfect duty.[5] That is the meaning of R2P, which asserts "the duties of governments to prevent and end unconscionable acts of violence against the people of the world, wherever they occur." States cannot turn a blind eye, even when acting "does not suit their narrowly defined national interests." In most cases, the survival of an intervening state is not at risk. So why shouldn't the obligation fall on the most capable state, the nearest or the strongest, according to the maxim "Whoever can, should"? Nonintervention in the face of mass murder or ethnic cleansing is not the same as neutrality in time of war. The moral urgencies are different; we are usually unsure of the consequences of a war, but we know very well the consequences of a massacre.

Still, if we follow the logic of the argument, it will be necessary to recruit volunteers for humanitarian interventions; the "who" who can and should is only the state, not any particular man or woman; for individuals the duty remains imperfect. Those deciding whether to volunteer may apply the same test to themselves— whoever can, should—but the choice is theirs. We might imagine a specially recruited UN force or an International Brigade of leftist fighters, though at this moment in the history of the United Nations and the left, those don't seem likely.

The justification of unilateralism that I have just provided is commonly questioned by leftists because they suspect the motives of single states acting alone. Won't such states act in their own interests rather than in the interests of humanity—or of the victims across the border? Yes, they probably will, or, better, they will act in their own interests as well as in the interests of the victims. I don't think it is particularly insightful, it is merely cynical, to suggest that those larger interests have no sway at all. Surely the balance of interest and morality among intervening states is no different from what it is among non-intervening states. In any case, how would humanity be better served by multilateral decision-making? Wouldn't each state involved in the decision also act in its own interests? Then the outcome would be determined by bargaining among the interested parties, and the desperate victims would not be one of the parties. We could hope that the particular interests would cancel each other out, leaving some kind of general interest (this is in fact Jean-Jacques Rousseau's account, or one of his accounts, of how citizens arrive at a "general will"[6]). But the bargain might reflect only a mix of particular interests, which may or may not be better for humanity than the interests of a single party.

Political motivations are always mixed, whether the actors are one or many. A pure moral will doesn't exist in political life, and we shouldn't require that kind of purity—or the pretense of it. We certainly shouldn't refuse to support intervention until a sufficiently disinterested actor arrives on the scene. The leaders of states (and, for that matter, the leaders of left-wing political parties) have an obligation to consider the interests of their own members even when they are acting to help other people. We should assume, then, that the Vietnamese had strategic reasons to invade Cambodia, that the Indians acted in their national interest when they assisted the secession of East Pakistan, and that Tanzania sent troops into Idi Amin's Uganda for reasons of its own. But these interventions also served humanitarian purposes and presumably were intended to do that, too. The victims of human-made disasters are very lucky if a neighboring state, or a coalition of states, has more than one reason to rescue them. It would be foolish to declare the multiplicity morally disabling. If the intervention is expanded beyond its necessary bounds because of some ulterior motive, then it requires critical scrutiny; within those bounds, mixed motives are a practical advantage.

Means

When the agents act, how should they act? Humanitarian intervention involves the use of force, and it must be pursued forcefully; the aim is the defeat of the people, whoever they are, who are carrying out massacres or ethnic cleansing. If these actions are awful enough to justify going in, they are awful enough to justify the pursuit of military victory. But this simple proposition hasn't found ready acceptance in international society, and it is the subject of frequent leftist criticism. Most clearly in the Bosnian case, there were repeated efforts to deal with the disaster without fighting against its perpetrators. Force was taken to be a last resort, but in an ongoing political conflict "lastness" never arrives; there is always something to be done before whatever it is that comes last. Military observers were sent into Bosnia to report on what was happening, then UN forces brought humanitarian relief to the victims, then they provided some degree of military protection for relief workers, and then they sought (unsuccessfully) to create a few safe zones for the Bosnians. But if soldiers do nothing more than these sorts of things, they are hardly an impediment to further killing; they may even be said to provide a kind of background support for it.[7] They guard roads, defend doctors and nurses, deliver medical supplies and food to a growing number of victims and refugees—and the number keeps growing. Sometimes it is helpful to interpose soldiers as peace-keepers between the killers and their victims. That may work for a time, but it doesn't reduce the power of the killers, which makes it a formula for trouble later on. Peacekeeping is an honorable activity, but not if there is no peace. Sometimes, unhappily, it is better to make war.

In Cambodia, East Pakistan, Uganda, and East Timor, the interventions were carried out on the ground; this was old-fashioned war-making. The Kosovo war provides an alternative model: a war fought from the air, with technologies designed to reduce (almost to zero!) the risk of casualties to the intervening army. I won't stop here to consider at length the reasons for the alternative model, which have to do with the reluctance of modern democracies to use the armies they recruit in ways that put soldiers at risk. In the old days, especially in colonial wars, the soldiers at risk were commonly from the "lower orders"—invisible, expendable citizens—or mercenaries hired for the occasion. In democratic states today, in principle at least, no such people are available, or if available, they are not similarly expendable, and in the absence of a clear threat to the community, there is little willingness to sacrifice lives for the sake of global law and order or, specifically, for the sake of Rwandans or Kosovars.

Inability and unwillingness, whatever their sources, make for moral problems. A war fought entirely from the air and from far away probably can't be won without attacking civilian targets. These need not be residential neighborhoods—they can be bridges, electric generators, and water purification plants—but the attacks will nonetheless endanger the lives of innocent men, women, and children. The aim is to bring pressure on a government acting barbarically toward a minority of its citizens by threatening to harm, or actually harming, the majority to which the government is presumably committed. This strategy wouldn't have worked against the Khmer Rouge in Cambodia, but even where it might work, it isn't legitimate if there is the possibility of a more precise intervention against the forces actually engaged in the barbarous acts. The same rules apply here as in war generally (and not only in wars we dislike): noncombatants are immune from direct attack and have to be protected as far as possible from "collateral damage." Soldiers have to accept risks to themselves in order to avoid imposing risks on the civilian population.

Any country considering military intervention will embrace technologies that lower the risks to its own soldiers, and the embrace is entirely justified so long as the same technologies do not increase the risks to civilians on the other side. This is precisely the claim made on behalf of "smart bombs" and missiles launched from drones. They can be fired from great distances, and they never miss. But the claim is, for the moment, greatly exaggerated. There is no technological fix currently available and therefore no way of avoiding this simple truth: from the standpoint of justice, you cannot attack a murderous government, with all the consequences that has for its citizens or subjects, while insisting that your own soldiers can never be put at risk. Once the intervention has begun, it may become morally necessary, if not militarily necessary, to fight on the ground—in order to win more quickly and save lives, for example, or to stop some particularly barbarous response to the intervention.

The moral argument against no-risk interventions seems to me very strong, but many leftists reject all arguments of this sort. They claim that the moral improvement of warfare only makes war more palatable and therefore more likely. But whenever war is necessary —to stop a massacre, for example—it is surely better that it be fought well. This means that positive steps must be taken to minimize civilian casualties, and sometimes these steps can only be taken by boots on the ground. A prudential argument also supports the moral argument: interventions must aim at political as well as military success, and these two together often require a visible willingness to fight and to take casualties. In the Kosovo case, if a NATO army had been in sight before the bombing of Serbia began, there might never have been the tide of desperate and embittered refugees. Postwar Kosovo would have looked very different; the tasks of policing and reconstruction would have been easier, and the odds of success much better.

Endings

Imagine the intervening army fully engaged. What should it consider victory? When is it time to go home? Should the army aim only at stopping the killing or at some further goal—destroying the military or paramilitary forces doing the killing, replacing the regime that employs these forces, or punishing the regime's leaders? Is intervention only a war or also an occupation? These are hard questions, and I want to begin my response by acknowledging that I have answered them differently at different times.

The answer that best fits the original legal doctrine of humanitarian intervention, the answer that is most likely to find support on the left and that I defended in *Just and Unjust Wars*, is that the aim of the intervening army is simply to stop the killing.[8] Its leaders prove that their motives are primarily humanitarian and that they have no imperial ambition by moving as quickly as possible to defeat the killers and rescue their victims and then leaving as quickly as possible. Sorting things out afterward, dealing with the consequences of the awfulness, deciding what to do with its agents—that is not properly the work of foreigners. The people who live there, wherever "there" is, must be given a chance to reconstruct their common life. The crisis that they have been through should not become an occasion for foreign domination. The principles of political sovereignty and territorial integrity require the "in and quickly out" rule.

On three sorts of occasions, however, this rule seems impossible to apply. The first is perhaps best exemplified by the Cambodian killing fields, which were so extensive as to leave behind no institutional base, and perhaps no human base, for reconstruction. I don't say this to justify the Vietnamese establishment of a satellite regime but rather to explain the need, years later, for the UN effort to create a locally legitimate political system.[9] The United Nations could not or would not stop the killing, but had it done so, the "in and quickly out" test would not have provided a plausible measure of success; it would still have been necessary to deal with the aftermath of the killing.

The second occasion is exemplified by all those countries— Uganda, Rwanda, Kosovo, and others—where the extent and depth of the ethnic divisions make it likely that the killings will resume as soon as the intervening forces withdraw. If the original killers don't return to their work, then their victims will take equally deadly revenge. Now "in and quickly out" is a kind of bad faith, a choice of legal virtue over political and moral effectiveness. If we accept the risks of intervention in countries like these, we had better accept also the risks of occupation (indeed, NATO forces are still at work in Kosovo).

The third occasion is the one I called nonstandard earlier on: where the state has simply disintegrated. It's not that the army or police has been defeated; security forces simply don't exist or are ineffective. The country is in the hands of paramilitary forces and warlords—gangs—who have been temporarily subdued. What is necessary now is to create a state, and the creation must be done virtually ex nihilo. That is not work for the short term.

In 1995, in an article called "The Politics of Rescue," published in *Dissent* magazine, I argued that leftist critics of the old protectorates and trusteeships needed to rethink their position, for these arrangements might sometimes be the best outcome of a humanitarian intervention.[10] The historical record makes it clear enough that protectors and trustees under the League of Nations again and again failed to fulfill their obligations; nor have these arrangements been as temporary as they were supposed to be. Still, their purpose can sometimes be legitimate: to open a span of time and to authorize a kind of political work between the "in" and the "out" of a humanitarian intervention. This purpose doesn't cancel the requirement that the intervening forces eventually get out. We need to think about better ways of making sure that the purpose is realized and the requirement finally met.

Perhaps this is where multilateralism can play a more central role than it has done in the original interventions. Multilateral occupations are unlikely to serve the interests of any single state and so are less likely to be sustained longer than necessary. The greater danger is that they won't be sustained long enough: each participating state will look for an excuse to pull its forces out. An independent UN force, not bound or hindered by individual states' political decisions, might be the most reliable protector and trustee—if we could be sure it would protect the right people in a timely way.[11] Whenever that assurance doesn't exist, unilateralism returns again as a justifiable option.

Yet we still need an equivalent of the "in and out" rule, a way of recognizing when a long-standing intervention has reached its end. The appropriate rule is best expressed by the idea of "local legitimacy." The intervening forces should aim at finding or establishing a form of authority that fits or at least accommodates the local political culture, and a set of authorities, independent of themselves, who are capable of governing the country and who command sufficient popular support that their government won't be massively coercive. The old regime failed in its Hobbesian obligation to protect the lives of its citizens; the military intervention should work to establish a new regime able to do just that. And once that regime is in place, the intervening forces should withdraw: "in and finally out."

But this formula may be as quixotic as "in and quickly out." Perhaps foreign forces can't do the work I have just described; they will only be dragged deeper and deeper into a partisan or sectarian conflict they can never control, gradually becoming indistinguishable from the other parties at odds. That prospect is surely a great disincentive to intervention; it will often override not only the benign intentions of potential interveners but even their strategic ambitions. In fact, intervention in most of the countries with inhabitants who desperately need rescuing offers little political or economic reward to the states that attempt the rescue. Leftist critics are surely wrong to suggest that such rewards are the only actual reasons for action. If the impure ambition of intervening states had more plausible objects, pursuit of those objects might hold them to their task. At the same time, however, it's important to insist that the task has limits: once the massacres and the ethnic cleansing are over and the people in command are committed to avoiding their recurrence, the intervention is finished. The new regime doesn't have to be democratic or liberal or pluralist or socialist. It only has to be a decent regime: non-murderous. When intervention is understood in this minimalist fashion, it may be a little easier to see it through.

As in the argument about occasions, minimalism in endings suggests that we should be careful in our use of human rights language —which is, and probably should be, the favorite language of the left. If we pursue the legal logic of rights (at least as that logic is understood in the United States), it will be very difficult for the intervening forces to get out before they have brought the people who organized the massacres or the ethnic cleansing to trial and established a new regime committed to enforcing the full set of human rights.[12] If those goals are within reach, then, of course, it is right to reach for them. But intervention is a political and military process, not a legal one, and it is subject to the compromises and tactical shifts that politics and war require. We will often need to accept lesser goals in order to minimize the use of force and the time span over which it is used. I want to stress, however, that we need, and haven't yet come close to, a clear understanding of what "minimum" really means. The intervening forces have to be prepared to use the weapons they carry, and they have to be prepared to stay a long course. The international community needs to find ways of supporting these forces and also, since what they are doing is dangerous and won't always be done well, of supervising and regulating them. And the rest of us should be ready to watch and criticize. That last task will be congenial to all varieties of leftists.

A Word about Civil War

I have been concerned with conflicts that take a relatively simple form: there are murderers, and there are victims. The murderers may be state officials, warlords, or populist mobs; the victims are almost all unarmed and helpless. But the last case on the list with which I started this chapter, Syria, is very different. What is going on there (as I write) is a civil war or, better, a Hobbesian "war of all against all"—in which there are unarmed victims but also contending armies or militias, all well armed, some more so than others. And there are multiple interveners, foreign powers, at odds with each other. I am sure the Syrian people would have preferred a unilateral intervention that defeated all the killers and stopped the killing. Instead they got a terrifying lesson in the dangers of multilateralism.

Military intervention in civil wars is most often not justified, for reasons originally provided by John Stuart Mill in his famous essay "A Few Words on Non-Intervention."[13] It is best, he argues, if the local balance of power determines the war's outcome. Self-determination of that sort may be brutal, but it is most likely to produce results that reflect the local culture and the commitments, active or passive, of most of the people. But even if states and armies should stay out, we leftists are not similarly constrained. In the Syrian case, we should have been in touch from the beginning with the protesters against the Assad regime. We should have been asking: How can we help? How can our unarmed NGOs join the struggle? There was even a moment early on when it was possible to think about an International Brigade.

Perhaps, after Iran and Hezbollah first entered the fight, we should have argued for the more active American role that our Syrian comrades, in Syria itself and in exile, were demanding. Mill's argument for non-intervention has this qualification: when one side receives forceful external help, it is permissible to help the other side. But the United States didn't provide the necessary help, or not enough of it; our Turkish and Saudi allies intervened in perverse ways; the Russians came in; and the war of all against all began. It doesn't appear (as I write) that the large-scale introduction of additional military forces could have helpful political or humanitarian effects.

What is necessary in cases like this one is a kind of bare humanitarianism and a very limited use of force—aimed at opening corridors to besieged cities, moving in supplies, creating safe zones, protecting medical personnel, and so on. I criticized just this kind of intervention in discussing the Bosnian case: it bandages the wounds but doesn't stop the wounding. But there may be times when there is nothing else to do, and the sheer awfulness of the Syrian war is probably an example. The wounded have to be saved even as the war goes on (but make sure the safe zones are really safe—they weren't in Bosnia).

Wars like this produce a flood of refugees who also have to be saved. Camps have to be established near the borders, with decent shelter and provision, and the host countries must be helped to bear the costs. And if nothing can be done to make it possible for the refugees to go home, plans for their resettlement have to be worked out. This is non-interventionist humanitarianism, not my subject here, but definitely a project that requires the engagement of left internationalists. That engagement should take a specifically leftist form. The aid organizations active in refugee camps do wonderful work, driven by a genuine sympathy for the people they are helping, but they tend to see these people as clients, as passive recipients of their help. As Killian Clarke has written, "Humanitarian organizations are not accustomed to recognizing the populations they care for as political actors." That recognition is what leftists can add to the "politics of refugee relief." Once again: an internationalism of agency.[14]

I have already commented on the support American leftists gave to the (far too few) Syrian refugees admitted to the United States. But there was no serious left campaign in support of Syrian protesters early on, or in support of a counter-intervention later, or, still later, in support of a limited use of force for strictly humanitarian purposes. There was no serious agitation for the commitment of significant resources to the men, women, and children fleeing the country. Nor, finally, was there at any point a willingness to talk to, and listen to, our Syrian comrades. We have to do better for Syria—and for the next Syria.

The Argument Reviewed

Let us return now to the more standard interventions, where foreign troops, sent at the right time, can stop the killing. I have tried throughout this chapter to answer objections to the argument that this is a good thing to do. But there are a couple of common criticisms of humanitarian intervention that I want to address more explicitly, even at the cost of repeating myself. I am going to take Edward Luttwak's critical review of Michael Ignatieff's *Virtual War* as a useful summary of the arguments I need to answer, since it is short, sharp, cogent, and typical.[15] Luttwak is no leftist, but he very forcefully makes arguments that I have most often encountered on the left. The book he is reviewing offers a stronger human rights justification of humanitarian warfare than I have provided, although Ignatieff would certainly agree that not every rights violation "shocks the conscience of humankind" and justifies military intervention. In any case, Luttwak's objections fail to meet either the arguments I have made here or Ignatieff's.

First objection: The "prescription that X should fight Y whenever Y egregiously violates X's moral and juridical norms would legitimize eternal war." But if we intervene only in extremity, only in order to stop mass murder and mass deportation, the idea that we are defending X's norms and not Y's is simply wrong. Possessive nouns don't modify morality in such cases. There isn't a set of different moralities for each X and Y in international society. The first proof of this is the standard and singular lie told by all killers and cleansers: they deny what they are doing; they don't try to justify it by reference to a set of private norms. Another proof is the overwhelming General Assembly vote for R2P.

Second objection: "Even without civil wars, massacres, or mutilations, the perfectly normal, everyday functioning of armies, police forces, and bureaucracies entails constant extortion, frequent robbery and rape, and pervasive oppression"—all of these, Luttwak claims, are ignored by the humanitarian interveners. So they are and should be, or else we would indeed be fighting all the time and everywhere. But Luttwak assumes now that the wrongness of the extortion, robbery, rape, and oppression is not a matter of X's or Y's private norms but can be recognized by anyone. Maybe he goes too far here, since bureaucratic extortion, at least, has different meanings and valence in different times and places. But the main actions on his list are indeed awful, and commonly known to be awful—even, I suspect, by post-modern cultural relativists. They just aren't awful enough to justify a military invasion. I don't think the point is all that difficult, even if we disagree about exactly where the line should be drawn. Pol Pot's killing fields had to be shut down, by a foreign army if necessary. The prisons of the world's more ordinary dictators should also be shut down. But that is properly the work of their own subjects—supported, I would hope, by the agitation of left internationalists.

Third objection: "What does it mean for the morality of a supposedly moral rule when it is applied arbitrarily, against some but not others?" The answer to this question depends on what the word "arbitrarily" means here. Consider a domestic example. The police can't stop every speeding car. If they go after only the ones they think they will be able to catch without endangering themselves or anyone else, their arrests will be "determined by choice or discretion," which is one of Webster's definitions of "arbitrary." But surely that determination doesn't undermine the justice of enforcing the speeding laws. On the other hand, if they only go after cars that have bumper stickers they don't like, and if their treatment of those drivers goes beyond what the law requires, making traffic control a pretext for the harrassment of political enemies or ethnic or racial minorities, then their actions "arise from will or caprice"—another definition of "arbitrary"—and are unjust. It's the first kind of arbitrariness that ought to (and often does) qualify humanitarian interventions. They are discretionary in this sense if prudential calculations shape the decision to intervene or not. Hence, as I have acknowledged, there won't be an intervention every time the justifying conditions for it exist. But to answer Luttwak's question, that acknowledgement doesn't affect the morality of the justifying rule. It's not immoral to act, or decline to act, for prudential reasons.

These three objections relate to the occasions for intervention, and rightly so. If no coherent account of the occasions is possible, then it isn't necessary to answer the other questions I have addressed. My own answers to the other questions can certainly be contested. But the main point I want to make is that the questions themselves cannot be avoided. Since there are legitimate occasions for humanitarian intervention, and since we know, roughly, what ought to be done, we have to argue about how to do it; we have to argue about agents, means, and endings. Many people on the left today (and on the right, too) want to avoid these arguments and postpone indefinitely the kinds of action they might require. These people have all sorts of reasons, but none of them, it seems to me, are good or moral reasons.

FOUR

Is There an American Empire?

The war in Iraq that began in 2003 and, after several metamorphoses, is still going on has given new urgency to the debate about "American imperialism." Yet there hasn't been anywhere near enough debate; the term has been used routinely by the war's critics and routinely rejected by its supporters. So is Washington the new Rome? Is there an American empire? Is Iraq an imperialist war? It seems to me that we need a better understanding of America's role in the world than this old terminology provides. Criticizing the uses of American power is a central political task, but it isn't our only political task. There are other countries and also, these days, non-state organizations whose use of power requires criticism; and there may be times when we want American power to be used.

Still, the easiest answer to my title question is, "Of course! Hasn't the United States played the major role in constructing a global market? Don't we control its regulatory agencies—the World Bank, the IMF, the WTO? Aren't most countries around the world open to the profit-seeking of American corporations and entrepreneurs?

Aren't "friendly" states with pro-business governments scattered around the globe?

But empire is a form of *political* domination, and it's not at all clear that market dominance and the extraction of profits require political domination. Perhaps they did in an earlier age—so the history of European empires and of the United States in Central America suggests. But the central claim of free marketeers today is that political domination isn't necessary, and this claim has been endorsed from the left by Michael Hardt and Antonio Negri in their opaque but highly popular book *Empire:* "The guarantee that Empire offers to globalized capital does not involve a micropolitical and/or microadministrative management of populations. The apparatus of command has no access to the local spaces and the determinate temporal sequences of life where the administration functions; it does not manage to put its hands on the singularities and their activity."[1] This is better understood in translation: "Empire" today does not mean what it once did. A twenty-first-century empire occupies no lands; it has no center (not even Washington); it doesn't depend on tightly controlled satellite governments; it is a post-modern entity.

Hardt and Negri's argument might be read as a (before the fact) response to people who claim that the Iraq war was from the start a war for oil. In reality, as the left has been saying for some time now, the control of natural resources does not require "access to local spaces" or the "microadministration" of territories and populations; it does not require colonies or satellites. The global market allows richer states to acquire and use the resources of poorer states—not independently of politics but without reliance on political domination. If the market didn't so successfully serve the interests of the rich, we would be much less critical of it than we are.

Some contemporary Marxists argue that what we have today is "an informal imperialism of free trade (or an imperialism without colonies)." But this argument entails, as an article by John Bellamy Foster in *Monthly Review* makes clear, a virtual identification of imperialism with capitalism: imperial power is simply "a manifestation of capitalist development in all its complexity." Its political forms, Foster says, are of only "secondary" importance.[2] That can't be right. If imperialism is nothing more than capitalism manifest and unfolded, if it has no independent and specifically political significance, then it isn't a useful term in political analysis. It can serve as a term of denunciation but not of enlightenment. I shall assume that imperialism is a system of political rule—not necessarily direct rule, but rule in some strong sense: an imperial power gets what it wants from the governments it creates, supports, or patronizes.

Is the United States politically dominant in this sense? We (Americans) are militarily powerful, overwhelmingly so. The British navy at the height of the British empire never came close to the firepower of the US Air Force today; nor could it deliver that firepower as quickly or as effectively around the world. It isn't clear, however, that firepower makes for imperial rule; even translating firepower into regional alliances or local collaboration is problematic these days. The old saying holds true: "You can do many things with a sword, but you can't sit on it." Modern military technology is no more comfortable. Despite the investment Americans have made in the most advanced weapons, the United States sometimes looks remarkably weak in the international arena, incapable of winning support for, let alone enforcing, our political policies—unless we go to war, which we can't do every time someone defies us. In any case, we aren't very good at winning our wars. We failed to defeat the Communists in Vietnam; we haven't been able to defeat the Taliban in Afghanistan or either the Sunni or Shi'ite militias in Iraq. Modern asymmetric warfare is very different from the old colonial wars that the well-armed colonial troops almost always won. In the years since our brutal destruction of the Philippine insurgency, America's high-tech army hasn't been able to win a war against low-tech militants fighting from civilian cover, often with support from compliant or terrified civilians.

American diplomats don't do much better. Their weakness was dramatically displayed in 2003, when the Turkish government refused to open the way for an invasion of Iraq from its territory. This was a newly elected government, chosen through the democratic procedures to which the United States is publicly committed, and we had no politically prudent way to bend the Turks to our will.

Equally noteworthy was the international opposition to the Iraq war. How can there be a global American empire if it is also true, as we were rightly told again and again in the left press, that the whole world was against us? Not only the people in the streets were against us but most of the world's governments, including our clients and allies, the provinces of our putative empire. If only two years after 9/11, on the eve of a major war, we could not count on states like Mexico and Chile to vote with us in the United Nations, what kind of empire did we have? (And Mexico and Chile have friendly governments; consider how many explicitly unfriendly, anti-American governments there are in what we used to think of as our southern "sphere of influence.") Nor, finally, has the United States been able to impose a regime of its choosing on Iraq—and here American diplomats had the advantage of what looked, for a brief while, like a decisive military victory. This is another example of what Dwight Macdonald, thinking of Vietnam, called an "inept" imperialism. But an imperialism so inept doesn't deserve the name.

Hegemony

"Empire" needs extensive qualification if it is to describe anything like what exists, or what is possible, in the world today. Hence the appeal of terms like Michael Ignatieff's "empire lite."[3] But perhaps there is a better way of thinking about contemporary global politics, drawing on the related idea of "hegemony." In common use today, "hegemonic" is simply a less vivid way of saying "imperialist," but it really points to something different: a looser form of rule, less authoritarian than empire is or was and more dependent on the agreement of others. Consider these words from Antonio Gramsci, the foremost theorist of hegemony—who wrote in the context of domestic political struggles: "The fact of hegemony presupposes that one takes into account the interests and tendencies of the groups over which hegemony will be exercised, and it also presupposes a certain equilibrium, that is to say that the hegemonic groups will make some sacrifices of a corporate nature."[4] Hegemony rests in part on force, but it rests also, even more importantly, on ideas and ideologies. If a ruling class has to rely on force alone, it has reached a crisis in its rule. To avoid that crisis, it has to be prepared for compromise.

In an essay on Gramsci, Stuart Hall provides a more extended analysis of the "multi-dimensional" character of hegemony (he is still writing about domestic politics):

> What "leads" in a period of hegemony is no longer described as a "ruling class" in the traditional language, but a historical bloc . . . The "leading" elements in a historical bloc may be only one fraction of the dominant economic class. . . . [A]ssociated with it, within the "bloc," will be strata of the subaltern and dominated classes who have been won over by specific concessions and compromises and who form part of the social constellation.[5]

Michael Bérubé comments usefully on this highly abstract passage: "The import is clear: mastery is not simply imposed or dominative in character; consent is not simply manufactured by a ruling class and its monopoly over the means of mental production."[6] The politics of a ruling class is largely internal, a matter of factions and intrigue; politics in a hegemonic system, by contrast, involves the interaction of independent actors, who must be drawn into a "bloc" through argument and concession. So the theory of hegemony provides a view of our political life that comes close to our everyday perception of its complexity.

Exactly how a similar analysis would work in international society isn't entirely clear, but hegemony would certainly require a more complicated understanding than the theory of imperialism allows. I don't have a fully developed alternative theory, only the beginning of an argument. Nor do I mean to suggest that America's recent rulers, who began the Iraq war, actually accepted the need for "sacrifices of a corporate nature" or for "concessions and compromises," even when they made them—as they did with the Turks in 2003 and as the Obama administration, more self-consciously, has done again with the Turks, and also with the Saudis, in the ongoing war against ISIS. President George W. Bush's unilateralism was a bid for dominance without compromise, which turns out to be impossible. But unilateralism hasn't been the natural mode of American power. Since World War II we (Americans) have played a major role in shaping international organizations; we have negotiated alliances, and we have generally been willing to consult with our allies in responding to critical events like the Iraqi invasion of Kuwait and in dealing (often reluctantly) with dangerous political or environmental tendencies like nuclear proliferation and global warming. The wish to act alone was an innovation of the second Bush administration—and was short-lived, or so it seemed, until the election of 2016. It was less the product of fear than of arrogance and ideological zeal, and it reflected a view of American power as inaccurate as that held by many of President Bush's critics. In the contemporary world, imperial rule is an exercise in futility—but a dangerous exercise nonetheless.

It is futile in the American case for three reasons. First, Americans don't have the stomach for old-fashioned imperialism. We are radically unready to pay the economic costs of empire—and empire, when it involves the "microadministrative management of populations," is expensive: there are profits for corporations like Bechtel and Halliburton, but only burdens for American taxpayers, who won't be willing to bear them for long. Nor will American mothers and fathers be willing to bear the costs in blood. We don't have an imperial army made up of "natives" and mercenaries. We have never created an imperial civil service; we don't even learn the languages or customs of the countries we mean to rule.

The American failure to impose law and order across Afghanistan, the deals the Pentagon made with local warlords (and then didn't enforce), our government's refusal to invest seriously in state-building outside Kabul: all this points not toward the skill and determination of imperial rule but toward the compromised character of hegemony—and also toward the amateurism of the American effort. Nor did our effort produce a particularly honorable version of hegemonic rule: it was hegemony without responsibility, which quickly came to mean no hegemony at all. Anyone who thought of the American engagement in Afghanistan as an imperialist war must have been surprised at its outcome. The United States lost men and material and gained none of the usual prizes of imperial rule. Nor is it clear that there was ever much to gain once the Cold War engagement with the Soviet Union was over. After 9/11, there were defensive reasons for the war, but imperialist reasons are very hard to find.

Ellen Willis argues strongly that the United States could have done good things in Afghanistan after the invasion—and I would add that there was also a debt to pay to the Afghans, given our role in bringing the Taliban to power. Here is Willis's argument:

> My frustration . . . is not that we took action in Afghanistan but that we have not done enough. We should have fought

the ground war and occupied Kabul; organized an international force to disarm the warlords, protect ordinary citizens, and oversee the distribution of aid; demanded that secularists be included in the negotiations for a new government and that basic women's rights be built into a new structure of law. If this is "imperialism"—in the promiscuous contemporary usage of that term— I am for it. I believe it is the prerequisite of a stable peace.[7]

I don't think Willis is actually advocating an imperialist program here; organizing her international force would have required a diplomacy of concession and compromise, and the gains she was looking for were definitely not material. This is a version of hegemony that the American left could support and should have supported. The actual conduct of the war and the under-resourced state-building that accompanied it required leftist criticism, but calling either of these imperialist didn't help anyone understand what was wrong with what we were doing.

The second reason for the likely futility of an American imperialism is that our public commitment to democracy makes imperial rule very hard to justify or manage. Even when that commitment is obviously hypocritical (for many years we supported non-democratic governments in countries like South Korea and Turkey), we do tend over time to encourage or enable or at least bear with democratic transformations. At the height of the Cold War, indeed, we refused to bear with democratically elected governments in Iran, Guatemala, and Chile. And possibly we will refuse in the future, in countries like Egypt, say, where radical Islamists rather than communists threaten to win elections. But it isn't easy for us to support dictators, even if they are "our" dictators; it produces a kind of legitimacy crisis for American power—another feature of hegemonic but not imperial rule.

The third reason for imperial futility is that under contemporary conditions, governments arise that are capable of opposing the imperialist policies of any aspiring great power. And then the aspiring power will, if it is wise, negotiate and compromise. In the world today, any refusal to do that, any full-scale imperialist project, would encounter such strong opposition from both large and small states, and so strong a sense among people everywhere that opposition was legitimate, that the project would be certain to fail.

When Rudyard Kipling called empire the "White Man's burden," he was stating, in the ideological idiom of his time, a simple fact: power brings responsibility. But the burdens of hegemony can't be borne alone; they have to be shared. A rationally governed hegemonic power doesn't act unilaterally to regulate trade, deal with rogue (or unfriendly) states, repel aggression, stop massacres, or take on the very difficult work of state-building; it seeks allies, it marshals coalitions. These will be coalitions of the willing, obviously, but the willingness has to be won by consultation, persuasion, and compromise. In the early 2000s, the US government sought to avoid any serious version of these necessary processes, as if its leaders wanted to manage the world all by themselves. That ambition is probably a better explanation of the Iraq war than any provided by the theory of imperialism. But America's leaders can't manage the world even when they are ready for consultation, persuasion, and compromise—as President Obama discovered. At the end of the Obama years, many of his critics asserted that the United States was no longer hegemonic. We had walked away from our responsibilities in, for example, the Middle East. That was a right-wing critique, but the thought that it might be true should have delighted many leftists. In fact, hegemony is still a useful description of America's place in the world.

A Note on Spheres of Influence

The Monroe Doctrine, which I described in chapter 1 as a defense of national liberation in South America, became by the end of the

nineteenth century a claim to an exclusive hegemonic role throughout the Americas. Theodore Roosevelt provided the classic reinter-
pretation: he insisted on the right of the United States to intervene
in cases of "flagrant and chronic wrongdoing" by a Latin American
nation.[8] The United States would, moreover, be the sole arbiter of
"wrongdoing." But Roosevelt did not claim literal imperial rule; the
Americas became a US "sphere of influence." All other countries
were to stay out; Americans alone could intervene. Of course, other
countries didn't stay out; the British were economically and politically engaged throughout the nineteenth century—as the Chinese
are today—and the United States didn't, and doesn't (because it
can't), force any of them out. But the US government did defend
against a French intervention in Mexico in the 1860s and against
the Soviet Union's attempt to provide military support for Cuban
communism a hundred years later. Indeed, the Monroe Doctrine
has been interpreted to allow the United States to oppose not only
foreign countries but anything that we consider a foreign or hostile
ideology.

The left has usually been critical—but not always: the defense
of Simón Bolívar and his friends would have been supported by
whatever passed for an American left in 1823, and most leftists,
such as they were in 1867, would probably have endorsed the effort
to remove the French-supported Maximilian I from his shaky Mex-
ican throne. Virtually all leftists supported the Castro revolution in
1959, but many had a hard time imagining the placement of Russian missiles in Cuba as an example of anti-imperialist politics. We
were, most of us, also opposed to the placement of American missiles in Turkey—so there was consistency here. But the removal of
both sets of missiles wasn't a defeat for hegemonic power. It might
be better described as the mutual recognition of two spheres of
influence.

Political "realists" accept spheres of influence as the natural product of military and economic power. The United States can exercise military power in Central America and the Caribbean; no one else can do that, so these areas fall within our sphere. The Russians once could, and can again, exercise military power in eastern Europe (as they did in Georgia in 2008 and more recently in Ukraine); no one else can do that or is willing to accept the entailed risks, so this part of the world, "realists" argue, belongs to them. The recognition of these spheres makes for political stability and enables the world to get on with business as usual. The Trump administration, in its early days, seems to be drawn to this kind of politics, in which great powers recognize each other's predominance over the lesser nations.

If this mutual recognition is merely a prudential argument about when to fight and when not to, it has undeniable force. Neither the United States nor the European Union was going to fight to defend the Georgian province of South Ossetia in 2008 or Ukrainian Crimea in 2016; nor should military action have been their response. No nation went to war for Hungary in 1956 or for Czechoslovakia in 1968. Military power has its practical prerogatives. Similarly, the Russians declined, very sensibly, to fight for Cuba in 1960—though it is worth noting that their refusal to fight did not lead to the overthrow of Cuban communism. Until 1989, the Russians ran an empire in eastern Europe, shaping and controlling each satellite state; American hegemony in Central America and the Caribbean was sometimes like that, but often not: again and again, anti-US politicians have prospered in our backyard.

For the left, ideally at least, military power has no prerogatives; it does not determine our moral or political positions. Most of the Western writers who have joined the debates about Georgia and Ukraine understand this, but, strangely, some people on the left have adopted something like the "realist" position about spheres of influence. They defend Russia's sphere, claiming that it makes for stability and peace and arguing that any strong Western commitment to, say, Ukraine's independence and territorial integrity is a threat to Russian security interests.[9] I want to sketch a better liberal-left approach to spheres of influence, keeping in mind the arguments I've already made about national liberation, state sovereignty, and hegemony. The easiest way to do that is to ask what or where the American sphere is and how we (leftists) should think about it.

It obviously doesn't include Georgia or Ukraine. But just as obviously, in any "realist" account, it does include Guatemala, Cuba, Nicaragua, and Panama—for starters. And yet, when the United States intervened in Guatemala in 1954 to overthrow the Árbenz government, I don't remember anyone on the left arguing that Guatemala was, after all, in our sphere of influence, and it would be best for global stability and peace if we had our way there. Nor did anyone I know on the left make an argument like that at the time of the abortive Bay of Pigs invasion of Cuba. Though a geographic stretch, Chile, too, has been widely thought (since the Monroe Doctrine) to lie within our sphere, and yet only right-wing cold warriors argued that the overthrow of Allende was a legitimate exercise of American influence. Liberals and leftists alike have been rightly critical of political exercises of that sort. Even those leftists who oppose populist politics did not support the US efforts, mostly unsuccessful, to undermine populist regimes in Central and South America. Hegemony in America's sphere hasn't been consistently maintained in recent decades, but it has been consistently criticized from the left.

Nonetheless, influence is a normal feature of political life. We all try to be as influential as possible. So how should influence work? When is it legitimate? What can a hegemonic power do—and when exactly should the left say no?

There is a line about this in Marx's *Economic and Philosophical*

Manuscripts. The line is focused on everyday social life and has never been invoked, as far as I know, in discussions of international politics. Assume, Marx writes, that our relation to the world is a "human" relation: "Then love can only be exchanged for love, trust for trust. . . . If you wish to enjoy art, you must be an artistically cultivated person; if you wish to influence other people, you must be a person who really has a stimulating and encouraging effect upon others."[10] I suggest that the case is the same with political parties, social movements, all sorts of NGOs, and with states, too. If they want to influence people in other countries, they must be stimulating and encouraging, which means materially helpful, politically supportive, ideologically persuasive. Marx's idea of "human" relations rules out coercion, manipulation, and subversion. Barring those three, influence isn't limited to a regional sphere—any person, any party or movement, any state can be influential anywhere.

Certainly there are moments—of massacre, ethnic cleansing, or religious persecution—when we should want our own country, and others, to seek a harder-edged influence. Major powers probably do have special responsibilities in their sphere (but not only there) to stop terrible things from happening—hence the right or obligation of humanitarian intervention that I defended in chapter 4 (which does not apply to just any "wrongdoing"). But influence should mostly depend on helpfulness and persuasion—which is another way of saying that the right of self-determination extends to all nations and peoples, whatever their geographic location. A leftist foreign policy should aim only at the "human" kind of influence—and the same policy is right for states, too, even hegemonic states.

If Russia wants to be influential in Ukraine, then it has to be helpful and persuasive to the Ukrainians: there is no other way. That, it seems to me, is the liberal and left position. "Realists" may be eager to recognize the kind of influence that is a function of military power, and political leaders may have to adapt to that kind of influence, at least for a time. But we, liberals and leftists, don't accept influence backed by arms as morally right or politically conclusive. Our parties and our movements should be active in other countries—building unions, training political activists, strengthening democratic institutions. We should work to undo imperial influence and foster "human" influence wherever we can, whether in the Caucasus or Chile. That work, indeed, is another way of defining what we mean when we call ourselves internationalists.

The Left and Hegemonic Rule

What kind of left politics follows from the more modest understanding of American power suggested by the idea of hegemony? In Britain in the first half of the twentieth century, leftists were "little Englanders"—that is, they advocated independence for the colonies. The United States is already committed, at least formally, to independence—that is, to the sovereignty of every existing state. After Iraq, even right-wing Americans are uninterested in microadministration. We are also formally committed to democracy. One thing the left can do is insist that these commitments be honored, not only in words but also in performance—both when the good and moral course of action compromises hegemonic power and when the good and moral course requires hegemonic power.

I will begin with the first of these possibilities. How many interests and tendencies, contrary to its own, is the American government ready to acknowledge and accommodate for the sake of global stability? What sort of equilibrium, with what other groups, is it willing to accept? Lenin once wrote that "the task of the intelligentsia is to make special leaders from among the intelligentsia unnecessary."[11] He didn't mean it, but the idea is useful. The task of a *democratic* hegemon is to make its own role less central, to make the exercise of power more and more consensual, more and more "human" in the young Marx's sense of that term.

I think the Obama administration tried to accomplish this—though not very successfully. It seems wise to assume that for the most part, most of the time, the goal of a better equilibrium, a more compromised hegemony, a more effective defense of democratic government, can be achieved only through left oppositionist politics. Leftists should be acting on this assumption: that we have a foreign policy to propose to the American people and that it differs from and stands in opposition to many features of the conventional foreign policy of American governments. So American leftists should be advocates of a self-limited hegemony. I don't mean to endorse the self-containment advocated by William Appleman Williams (see chapter 1), which is a version of the default position: improving life at home and staying away from engagements abroad. Instead, self-limitation should be the beginning of activism abroad. Latin America is the obvious place to start, with the 2015–2016 accommodation with Cuba as a useful example. Re-establishing diplomatic relations with Cuba was advocated for many years on the left, even by leftists who were at the same time critical of the Cuban regime; it is an example of looking for the right sort of influence in our sphere of influence. Self-limitation as activism would also mean signing on to (and upholding) instruments like the ABM treaty, strengthening the Kyoto and Paris climate agreements, and joining the International Criminal Court. It would mean promoting greater mutuality in world trade, opening our doors wider to imports from the poorer countries of the world, and urging other wealthy nations to do the same. All these moves would involve qualifications of hegemony, the acceptance of universal rules equally applied, and hence would constitute sacrifices of a corporate nature. As Gramsci suggests, however, these sacrifices don't eliminate hegemonic power: they modify it in ways useful to humanity, but they also represent a form of intelligent maintenance.

Another example of self-limitation that leftists should be working for is greater transparency in the use of American military power around the world—and greater democratic control of that power. The so-called War on Terror is mostly police work, some of which probably has to be done in secret. But the rules of engagement for this work should not be secret, and leftists should be as engaged in debates about the application of those rules abroad as we are in debates about their application at home. That the police require scrutiny and criticism is an easy left position; that they sometimes require support is harder. The same applies when the War on Terror becomes an actual war, involving preemptive strikes against terrorist groups and individuals in faraway places: scrutiny and criticism are always necessary, and so, sometimes, is support.

Probably the most dramatic manifestation of US hegemony is that we are the only country able to deploy military force across the globe. But US deployments have not been subject to democratic review and debate—as they should be. There are, indeed, leftists who have adopted the anti-American shortcut I described in chapter 1 and who demand an end to all the deployments. No doubt, anti-Americanism has its reasons. In the years after 9/11 it seemed as if the American obsession with guns at home had spilled over into an obsession with the use of force abroad. The United States fought its wars in Afghanistan and Iraq without any serious commitment to the political and diplomatic work that war requires. Still, taking the anti-American shortcut means refusing the politics of distinction. There are real enemies out there, some of whom are enemies not only of America but of large swaths of humanity—particular ethnic groups, minorities of different sorts, secular democrats, feminists, religious heretics, infidels. These vulnerable people often look to the global hegemon for help—and sometimes what they need is more than stimulation and encouragement. There are many right-wing "realists" who don't want to help; leftists should not march with them.

Does hegemonic power require endless war? This is a standard critique of the War on Terror, but I think it is misplaced. The police work that makes up most of this war is indeed endless—though perhaps not quite as literally endless as the war on crime. We can imagine religious zealotry in decline and key political conflicts approaching resolution—and then there would be a significant reduction in terrorist attacks. But at this moment there is no visible endpoint, and insisting that there should be one doesn't make sense. Leftists should insist instead on the need for democratic debate about each engagement of American forces abroad. And when we join these debates, we need to take into account the views of comrades abroad—democrats, secularists, feminists—who may or may not support those engagements.

The same argument holds with regard to the massive export of weapons by the US government and by private American companies. This, too, should be subject to democratic review and regulation—and here, again, the politics of distinction applies. Not all arms exports are wrong. Remember the demand of the international left in the 1930s that France, Britain, and the United States sell arms to the Spanish Republic. There are countries that need weapons to defend themselves against threatening neighbors. But we should definitely not be arming the threatening neighbors. Nor, obviously, should we be arming governments that oppress their own people.

Hegemonic power, in all its versions—material, political, and military— can be a force for good in the world, or at least a useful force against many kinds of badness. Some leftists dream of an egalitarian world order in which states are far more equal in power and wealth than they are today, and some versions of anti-Americanism may spring from that dream. But opposition to American hegemony is not, nor can it realistically be, opposition to hegemony itself. There will be other hegemons, and not necessarily better ones. An intelligent leftism should aim to make sure that American power is used well—which means distinguishing among its possible uses. Imagine, for example, the role that the United States could have played, but didn't, by calling for a UN response to the Rwanda massacre and providing logistical support for military action to stop the killing. Or, consider the US role in the Kosovo intervention—not a perfect example, but important in this sense: no other country could have led that intervention. Or, consider the role we could have played in Central American economic development had we not been perversely engaged in defense of US companies and corporations; or the role we could now play in dealing with the global refugee crisis if we didn't have an actively xenophobic government.

American leftists, accustomed to opposing US actions in places like Guatemala and Chile, must learn to acknowledge alternative possibilities. This may mean urging American governments with too narrow a conception of the national interest to engage in humanitarian work. Or it may mean demanding limits on, or simply opposing, government policies that smack of imperial arrogance and ambition. We also need to insist that benign uses of hegemonic power depend on the help of other states and that self-limitation of that power may also need the balancing work of others. We should be advocates of a global division of political labor.

So let us consider again Gramsci's idea of an equilibrium whose international version might be an old-fashioned balance of power between the hegemonic state and some set of rival states. China and Russia are playing this role in parts of the world—and playing it in ways that suggest their own arrogance and ambition. They certainly set limits on American hegemony, but from a left point of view, it is more useful to imagine a Gramscian equilibrium in the form of a US-EU partnership. America needs a partner who can say yes and no, who can act with the United States sometimes and independently at other times. But if such a partnership is to be established and sustained, European states would have to resolve their current divisions and defeat the populist and nationalist movements that threaten their unity. Right now, the European Union doesn't seem prepared to take responsibility or share responsibility for the way things go in the world.

But we should hope for sharing; we should hope that European states take on some of the work the hegemon does (some of which is necessary work). The more responsibility they accept, the more the hegemon would have to negotiate and compromise, the more the equilibrium would shift toward equality. Had Europe—for example—dealt forcefully and effectively with the crisis of the former Yugoslavia without involving the United States, America would be less hegemonic than it is today.

It would certainly help the American left if there were leftists in Europe advocating forceful and effective foreign policies. Back in the 1980s, the British socialist Michael Rustin argued that Europeans could not assert their independence vis-à-vis the Americans so long as they were "toothless" participants in arms negotiations. They needed to take responsibility for their own defense and cooperate in "both the resourcing and the command of their forces."[12] Rustin's argument pertained only to the defense of Europe, but after the Balkan wars of the 1990s, European leftists should also support the creation of forces capable, independently of the United States, of stopping mass murder and ethnic cleansing—not only in Europe but elsewhere. Right now, that support would require oppositionist politics within the European left itself.

Another kind of oppositionist politics might arise within international civil society. I have said this already: states are not the only actors in the world today. Multinational corporations, which play a major part in the global economy, are the central agencies of Hardt and Negri's decentered Empire. Multinationals are an unlikely source of opposition to hegemonic power, although they might set themselves against imperial recklessness. More important for my purposes here are the new and proliferating nongovernmental organizations that defend universal values or collective interests and play a still-to-be-defined part in global politics. Hardt and Negri deny the oppositionist potential of these organizations, citing the role human rights NGOs played in Bosnia and Kosovo, where their "moral intervention [became] a frontline force of imperial intervention."[13] But this argument seems radically wrong, given the moral necessity of those particular interventions and the great difficulty of fitting them into any coherent theory of imperialism. Organizations like Human Rights Watch and Amnesty International can intervene not only at the margins of empire but also at its center— as they did in the case of the Soviet Union and its satellites. Today they can address themselves to human rights violations in countries "over which hegemony is exercised" and also in the United States itself. They provide a good example of Marx's "human" influence.

Since the global market is the primary ground of American hegemony, we have to imagine NGOs that work through or against regulatory agencies like the World Trade Organization and that aim to constrain the power of capital—in the way domestic social-democracy did in the nineteenth and twentieth centuries. The 1999 protests at the WTO's Ministerial Conference in Seattle offered the barest intimation of what that kind of political work might look like, and there hasn't been any significant follow-up in the years since. We don't yet know whether international civil society will provide space and opportunity not only for human rights and environmentalist groups, and other single-issue organizations, but also for global movements with large redistributive ambitions. Here Hardt and Negri are more optimistic than I am, but the question I raised in chapter 2—Is a cross-border social-democracy possible?— is surely the crucial question about the future of hegemonic power.

Meanwhile, when we look for a new equilibrium in the society of states or for new social movements in international civil society, we need to understand that we are not organizing a revolt of the imperial provinces. We need to construct a different kind of politics, adapted to the real power, but also to the characteristic looseness, of hegemonic rule. Writing in the months just before the Iraq war, Martin Walker described this looseness under the name "virtual empire." I don't much like the name, for the equilibrium I am looking for isn't virtual or imperial. But Walker's description, despite being written from the side of the hegemon and nowhere near as critical as it should be, can help us understand the new reality. He failed to anticipate the high-handedness of the Bush administration, but he did anticipate the style of President Obama's diplomacy. The virtual empire, he wrote, maintains its preeminence "with more than a degree of courtesy for the rest of the international order." Allies are treated with the respect due to sovereign states. Former enemies (like Russia after 1989) are invited and helped to become new friends, and when this fails, they are engaged "coldly," that is, diplomatically and economically, without military heat. The rulers of the virtual empire can be harsh in defending their interests and sometimes also the interests of others, but at the same time, their policies are "open to argument and persuasion" from foreign states, corporations, and interest groups of many different kinds— and also, obviously, from the left. The American virtual empire "is a new beast," Walker concludes, "the like of which the world has not seen before."[14] Whatever we call the beast and whatever we say about it, we had better recognize its newness.

Any effort from the right to "make America great again" will only expose the wobbly character of hegemonic rule and the constant need for compromise and conciliation. Confident claims from the left that America is in full political and economic control, that we leftists are in full intellectual control, and that all we have to do is apply Lenin's theory of imperialism (which we all know by heart)—this, too, is an invitation to political failure.

FIVE

Global and Domestic Justice

As I argued in the introduction, domestic justice is the first commitment of the left; it is the project with which we have always been most effectively engaged. When we look abroad, we are inclined to focus on issues like those that we grapple with at home: sweatshop factories, anti-union practices, tyrannical managers, and so on. But we also need to think about the larger distributive issues and the gross inequalities across international society. And we can't—for reasons I will describe—aim at exactly the same kind of justice abroad that we aim at domestically. So what should justice abroad mean to men and women of the left, and what efforts should it inspire?

Global justice would seem to require a global theory—a single philosophically or ideologically grounded account of what justice is that explains why it ought to be realized in exactly this way, everywhere, right now. Many people on the left—and many liberals, too—look for such a theory or, better, for a comprehensive and compelling story about the just society, about equality, liberty, international trade, mutual aid, and much else—a story that need only be repeated again and again, for it applies identically to every country in the world, even to every person, and calls for a straight-forward linear realization.

There are several well-known difficulties with this project. First, there is no one to tell the story to who can act authoritatively in its name. There is no global agent of justice comparable to the ruling class of a modern state or its democratically elected government. Marxists once believed that the international working class or the proletarian dictatorship would become the global agent, but right now there is no reason to believe that anything like that is possible. Nor is there an alternative set of agents, states, or NGOs whose legitimacy is widely recognized, who might take up the story in its one true version and pursue the project it describes. The members of the UN Security Council are obviously unwilling and unable to undertake any such effort.

Second, even those who agree that there ought to be a single comprehensive story end up telling different stories. Old leftists believed in the existence of an ideologically correct position but never agreed on what it was. There are cosmopolitan and statist versions, revolutionary and reformist versions, even religious and secular versions—and each version has its own storytellers (and philosophers) who insist that theirs is the one true version.

Third, we can't be sure that whatever story we tell will be un-derstood in the same way by everyone who hears it—or that it will be understood in the way the storytellers intend. The story won't connect with a universal common life with interests and ideals that might make it comprehensible and then appealing. There are many common lives of different sorts but no common life of that sort. The diversity of cultures and the plurality of states make it unlikely that any one account of justice could ever be persuasive or enforce-able across the globe. A global despot (if sufficiently enlightened) or an ideological vanguard might manage the enforcement, but it is hard to see how that enforced rule, even if it served the cause of justice, could itself be just.

And yet the world's vast inequalities of wealth and power, and the accompanying poverty, malnutrition, and illness, cry out for a globally applicable critique. So does the extreme vulnerability of so many people to natural disaster and political violence—not only in the third world but also in the first and second. Moreover, the critique cannot endorse the idea that cultural difference makes a difference; it must insist on the simple wrongness of the human suffering we currently live with and, mostly, accept. If we force ourselves to look, the picture is grim: extraordinary wealth and terrible poverty, the powerful few and the powerless many, tyrants and warlords and their desperate victims, transnational corporations and oppressed workers, those who live in mansions and those who live in squalor, diners on haute cuisine and scavengers for garbage. These polarities are frightening and, from a left perspective, obscene. But it is the people at their farther, grimmer end whose living conditions and daily deaths demand from leftists, and from everyone else, a single coherent moral and political response. We don't need to agree on the absolute wrongness of inequality, or on a complete list of human rights, or a full-scale theory of distributive justice in order to support a global campaign against poverty, hunger, and disease, against mass murder and ethnic cleansing.

No doubt, each of these human disasters is at least partly the product of local causes and local agents, but they are also the products of an international economy increasingly marked by the flow of money, labor, and goods across political and cultural boundaries and of an international politics increasingly marked by the use of force and the transfer of military resources across those same boundaries. We (leftists and everyone else) need to attend to what goes on within particular states, cultures, and religions, but we need first to address the kind of suffering that has only a human face. Here global impact takes precedence over local difference.

How, then, should we address the terrible injuries endured by the people at the wrong end of the global polarities? How should we think about the urgent needs of the desperately poor and the desperately weak? What policies should we be pressing on their behalf? The first thing to recognize is the broadness of that "we." Global justice begins as a human, not a leftist, project; the particular work of the left comes later.

So let's agree that there is no near prospect of a globally accepted comprehensive theory and that, right now, there is no globally effective agent who could put such a theory into practice—and "right now" is the absolutely necessary temporal rule. What we require to meet the needs of the hour is minimal: recognition that other people are like ourselves, sympathy with their suffering, and a few widely shared moral principles. If these amount to a theory, it is a little theory, incomplete in much the same way that global society is incomplete. It can do only a few things, and do them only in a rough and ready way: its realization depends on the uncoordinated activities of many different agents. This minimalist account of justice-right-now has two aspects; the first is humanitarian and is everyone's work; the second is political, the work of the left. I will examine them in that order. What will remain to be done once justice-right-now is realized (if it ever is), what kind of justice lies beyond our current urgencies, and how just institutions and practices might be developed and sustained—together these require a maximalist theory of a fairly complex sort, adapted to the realities of cultural and political difference. I will say something later on about those realities and about the pursuit of justice-over-the-long-run.

The Humanitarian Project

Most of us, when we see human beings suffering, feel a natural empathy and want to help—unless, as Rousseau says in his "Discourse on the Origin of Inequality," we have been corrupted by philosophy. The American philosopher John Rawls, who raises a powerful voice against that kind of corruption, claims that there is a natural duty to help people in trouble—a "duty of mutual aid."[1] He is right, I think, and this duty must have its root in fellow feeling, in the intuitive recognition of "others" as people like us. It is this natural empathy that explains the outpouring of aid after a devastating flood or earthquake. The response comes from thousands of ordinary men and women acting through voluntary associations (NGOs), as well as from political communities (states) acting in the name of their citizens. But it starts from the feelings of individuals. How can feelings generate a duty? It must be because one of the things we feel is that we ought to feel this way: we ought to want to help.

We think of floods and earthquakes as natural disasters, but we know their effects are often aggravated by malevolent or negligent human agents. Similarly, many of the disasters of social life were once imagined to be acts of nature, but these days we are inclined to look for direct or indirect human agency. In all these cases, whether the suffering is caused by nature or by human action, it is right to act out of fellow feeling, to respond in a humanitarian way. But whenever human agency is involved, we are also required to follow the causal chain to identify the agents. We have to examine the history of malevolence or negligence and consider the responsibilities of all the men and women in the chain—including ourselves. Once we know the names of the agents, natural duty may well be seconded by, or transformed into, political obligation.

But we have to begin with the natural duty to relieve human suffering. We don't do this very effectively for several reasons: there is so much suffering; it has so many different causes; and no single organized relief effort exists. Still, in particular cases, we ought to help as best we can, and these cases extend beyond singular events like floods and massacres to encompass general conditions like deep poverty, homelessness, endemic disease, and ongoing persecution and repression. I am going to focus mostly on poverty in this chapter because the poor suffer the most from every other kind of disaster. Americans saw this very clearly when hurricane Katrina destroyed much of the city of New Orleans. It was the poorest residents who lived on the lowest ground, who were protected by the least well-maintained levees, whose homes suffered the greatest damage. This is, as we all know, a common story. Disease kills the weak and the malnourished first. Earthquake and fire are most deadly for those who live in flimsy houses and tenements. Even a disaster like ethnic cleansing, where the violence cuts across class lines, has its cruelest impact on people without the resources to escape. We can take poverty as the primary condition of human suffering—the first humanitarian crisis, the first object of our natural duty to help.

Again, we ought to help for simple humanitarian reasons, and we don't need a theory of justice to do this—though plausible theories about economic and political causation would certainly help. We will also find helpful, as David Miller has argued, a theoretical account of the assignment of responsibility, or at least primary responsibility, in a given case.[2] But what ought to be done, concretely, here and now, is often far from obvious, even when we agree on who should do it. We are bound to argue about which is the best remedial policy, to try to identify a set of possibly useful policies, and to press the appropriate agents to carry them out. Some of these agents will be NGOs, some will be attached to religious communities, some will be UN-sponsored, but the most effective agents in a global society of states are the existing states. That means that even our humanitarian efforts require political action; we have to press for the engagement of state officials and the expenditure of state money.

Because we think of these efforts as humanitarian, the duty to join them extends to all humanity. The duty of individuals, and of their associations, including their states, is commensurate only with their ability to help; it is a universal duty, and I think we experience it that way. We may feel a deeper empathy or a greater urgency in the case of ethnic kin or fellow believers, and that connection, as Miller says, is one reason to assign (primary) responsibility for their rescue or relief. It is not unjust, as some leftists believe, to feel especially obligated to neighbors and kinfolk. Still, the sight of suffering, whoever the victims are, brings with it a duty to respond. I know that many people don't feel this duty, but enough of us do (and we, too, are many), and we feel bound not just as individuals but as members of, even on behalf of, humanity as a whole. When we give money to Oxfam, or to Doctors Without Borders, or to Human Rights Watch, or when we ask the US government to send the navy (grateful at that moment that we have a navy) to help the victims of a tsunami, we are simply doing what we ought to do.

Exactly how much individual men and women are required to give of their time, energy, and money I am not able to say; nor can I or anyone else instruct individuals about how to choose the disasters to which they devote their resources. The allocation of governmental resources also requires difficult choices. There are certainly arguments to be made for doing this rather than that—the urgency of the case, say—but we must not expect definitive theoretical guidance. It is probably possible, though, and if it's possible, then it is also necessary, to insist that individuals and states do more, even if we cannot specify exactly how much they should be doing. Hence the effectiveness of Thomas Pogge's argument that it would take only a very small percentage of the wealthiest countries' GDP to end global poverty.[3] If that is true, then there is a strong argument for deploying those resources, whatever other deployments might be morally required.

Sometimes, in cases of human-created disasters like massacre or

ethnic cleansing, or in the case of political famines (caused or sustained for reasons of state), the necessary response involves the use
of force. In chapter 3, I defended humanitarian intervention against
leftist objections—without, however, claiming it as a leftist project.
It is, like all forms of humanitarianism, a universal duty. The obligation to stop a massacre falls on anyone, that is, on any state or
coalition of states, capable of acting effectively. Individuals are not
capable in such cases, and NGOs sometimes provide relief for the
wounded, as I argued above, in ways that actually facilitate the ongoing killing. Forceful state action is required here; the goal is to
stop the massacre and then to help install a non-murderous regime.
Once again, the leaders of a military intervention don't require a
theory of the best regime to guide their efforts; they, too, should be
minimalists. Nor is military force necessary in most humanitarian
crises—not in the standard refugee crisis and certainly not in the
crisis of poverty, where nonviolent responses like the commitment
of resources and the mobilization of trained personnel are the only
ones likely to be useful.

The Left's Political Project

Humanitarian responses should be the same whether the crisis is a
natural disaster or the product of human action (or inaction). Our
natural and universal duty is to relieve the suffering. Whoever can,
should. That's not a complete assignment of responsibility, but it
is the necessary beginning. If we examine the suffering caused by
human beings, we will be led to argue for more particular obligations. Much of the world's poverty and many of poverty's attendant
disasters are caused by predatory rulers, corrupt oligarchs, and brutal warlords. These are the agents of political plunder, economic
disruption, civil war, and mass flight. They are not, however, the
sole agents, for many of them are assisted or supported by more
distant and less visible political and economic actors. States seeking

reliable allies, offering to sell weapons and train police; corporations looking for cheap labor or hoping to avoid regulation; entrepreneurs bribing public officials and living beyond local law; banks eager to receive the plundered money—these, too, are agents of human disaster.

Since some of these agents are acting on America's behalf—defending national security, say, or providing Americans with cheap consumer goods or with spectacular (if sometimes risky) investment opportunities—responsibility for their actions extends to US citizens generally. The same argument applies to the citizens of other wealthy and powerful states. The relevant moral principle is as obvious (and as often ignored) as the principle of mutual aid: You must help undo injuries to other people that you helped to cause—whether the help consisted in acting or failing to act. This remedial work is a specifically leftist project.

There are so many examples of complicity in human disaster that it seems arbitrary to illustrate my argument with just one. Paul Collier, the author of *The Bottom Billion*, describes some of the ways Western governments and corporations help to sustain the deep poverty of the worst-off people in the world. He asks us to consider the role of Western banks when poor countries experience revenue booms from oil or other mineral resources. Much of the money is siphoned off by local elites, often with the help of the extracting companies, and sent to banks in the West. What do the banks do then? "Basically," writes Collier, "they keep quiet about it. Is this a necessary consequence of banking secrecy laws? No, it is not. If the money is suspected of having terrorist associations . . . we now require the banks to blow the whistle on it. But if it is stolen from the ordinary citizens of the bottom billion, well, that is just too bad."[4] Vast amounts of money have in fact been stolen—enough, if the funds had been well spent, to make at least a dent in the deep poverty of the poorest countries.

I don't suppose we have a natural duty to work for the reform of the banking system. But doing so is obligatory work for leftists who live in the countries that the banks serve and who themselves benefit from the service—and we must try to enlist our fellow citizens in the work. The obligations of bank officials and state regulators are certainly more substantial and easier to specify. Those of ordinary citizens are weaker and more diffuse, but they still have some claim on us. And there are likely to be many similar obligations: to oppose assistance from our own government to predatory regimes; to support the political and economic reconstruction of countries devastated by civil wars that our country instigated or in which it intervened; to change trade policies that discriminate against the products of poor countries; to stop the competitive "race to the bottom" in labor costs; to require powerful transnational corporations based in our country to pay minimum wages, protect the environment, observe safety laws, and recognize independent unions when they operate in other countries—even if the governments of those other countries are too weak or corrupt to maintain a regulatory regime.

In sum, we need to oppose the neo-liberal version of a global economy, manifest in recent trade agreements and economic unions that enshrine the laissez-faire trinity: the free movement of capital, commodities, and labor. Many people on the left, especially those committed to the one true story of global justice, believe that open borders are a key feature of a just world order. Maybe so, but only if this world order includes a world government capable of providing the full range of social-democratic regulations that domestic laissez-faire first made necessary. No such government exists today or is likely to exist anytime soon. The free movement trinity constitutes a capitalist paradise, but it leaves far too many people unprotected and consigned to a capitalist hell. Since we are complicit in the consignment, we have work to do.

The list of things that need to be done is very long, and so, again, leftists will have to make difficult choices about where to direct our energies. It is a feature of organizational life in liberal democracies that many agents —political parties, social movements, labor unions, religious groups, NGOs of different sorts—work on issues like these. Global civil society contains similar organizations that can raise money in democratic countries and then work, though not without risk for their workers, in countries ruled by tyrants or torn apart by warring gangs or feverish sects. We can meet our obligations in many different ways and in many different places.

But, it might be argued, people are not going to take action in sufficient numbers for the project to succeed. Reparative justice as a political project is no less utopian than comprehensive global justice. Even if the resource transfers we defend are smaller than those required by a comprehensive theory of justice, they are still too large to command wide support among the citizens of the richer countries. That may be so, but I suspect that the transfers are considerably smaller than the standard comprehensive theories and correct ideological positions would require. What is equally important, they follow from principles of mutual aid and political responsibility that are widely accepted even when the transfers themselves are resisted. This means that there are political battles that can be fought and won—or partly won. The cause of justice-right-now can be incrementally advanced.

Well, then, critics might continue, can't a more comprehensive justice also be incrementally advanced by exactly the same means, and shouldn't leftists aim at the larger goal? The defeat of predatory rulers, the reconstruction of devastated countries, the reform of the banks, fair trade, and the regulation of transnational corporations—wouldn't all this also be required by any theory of comprehensive justice? It probably would, but if all this is achieved by many states and NGOs, working independently with varying success, then it may not in fact advance a comprehensive scheme. Indeed, the very success of justice-right-now will make comprehensiveness more difficult.

That last point needs further explanation. One of the goals of justice-right-now, in both its humanitarian and its political aspects, is to provide people around the globe with sufficient resources to act on their own behalf. This is what I called in chapter 2 an internationalism of agency. Relief after a devastating flood, for example, should aim at allowing people not only to resume a more or less normal life but also to work with water engineers and state officials to prevent future floods. When we force banks to give up the plundered money of tyrants and warlords, we are hoping for the emergence of states that can invest that money in education and development. When we argue for fair trade, we are aiming at the creation of local economies capable of providing jobs and security. When we support political reconstruction after civil wars and massacres, we are trying to create regimes ready and able to protect the lives of all their citizens. The natural duty and the political obligation to aid disaster victims have this corollary: we should not deal with disasters in ways that make it likely that we will have to deal with them again and again. We help people to make them better able to help themselves.

The crucial agent of self-help in the world today is the state—I mean a decent state, controlled by its citizens, acting on their behalf, defending their rights and interests. It might be a good thing if there were international agencies that monitored, reported on, and regulated the activities of states, but no such agencies exist today. The United Nations sometimes claims this role, and some of its agencies work effectively to improve the quality of life of the world's inhabitants, but no state officials would voluntarily entrust the well-being of their people to the United Nations as it currently exists. NGOs like Human Rights Watch and Amnesty International

provide scrutiny and reporting, but they have no regulatory powers. Justice-right-now works only in and through the sovereign or
semi-sovereign states of the global order.

If these states succeeded in maintaining peace and security, preventing flood and famine, providing education and welfare, plan-
ning economic development, and policing foreign investors, they
would make the world more just. But success would not necessarily
advance the cause of global justice if it is conceived in terms of
a single comprehensive theory. This is so for two reasons. First,
people living in the countries that contributed significant resources
to relief and repair, and hence to the success just described, might
feel they were now entitled to focus on the problems of their own
society—given that everyone else was able to do that too, though
still with unequal resources. Second, a local focus would not produce anything like convergence on a single uniform system of distributive justice. A free politics in many different states would result
instead in many different versions of welfare, taxation, economic
regulation, and public and private ownership.

The Struggle for Domestic Justice

How, then, should we think about justice-over-the-long-run?[5] Relief and repair will create a world considerably more egalitarian
than today's world. Beyond that, I don't think leftists need to insist
on universal and absolute equality. If men and women everywhere
were protected from the common disasters of nature and social life,
if the predatory versions of politics and economics were under control, if decency was common across the globe, we could let cultural
difference, political struggle, and economic competition work their
way and produce . . . whatever they produce.

I don't mean that whatever they produce will be all right or
good enough or even good at all. We will still require strenuous
social criticism and, even more important, repeated political strug-

gle. But these will now be local and reiterative across the globe. In a famous line the Bible tells us, "Justice, justice shalt thou pursue" (Deuteronomy 16:20). But the relevant "thou," once the world has achieved economic sufficiency and political decency, is not humanity as a whole but rather the plurality of human communities. Let there be many pursuits. Let a hundred flowers bloom. It is a tribute to human creativity that communities, cultures, and religions should have different ideas about the relative value of different social goods and about the distributive criteria appropriate to each. There will be different priorities and understandings even within the same community, culture, or religion: difference and disagreement are universal features of human life. But there are common fields of reference, common histories and literatures, and common commitments that give a particular shape to human disagreements. These commonalities tend to be reproduced within political communities through highly differentiated cultural and religious institutions. When the commonalities extend across political boundaries—as they do, or as we once thought they did, in the case of the European Union—the pursuit of justice should be extended in the same way. If the commonalities were ever to extend across the globe, we would need only a single pursuit of a uniform and comprehensive justice (assuming that we could reach agreement on what that is). But regional extension is rare today, and global extension is nonexistent. We see faint signs of its emergence with regard to some social goods—as in the universal lip service paid these days to the democratic distribution of political power. But lip service is far short of commitment, and global understandings of other social goods are remarkable in their divergence.

Global justice ought to be a response to urgent need, to the suffering of the worst-off, the victims of natural disaster and human depredation, the poor and the powerless. Its two necessary aspects are mutual aid in time of crisis and political responsibility for injuries across borders. Its time constraint is *right now*. But the long-term distribution of social goods among people who have been freed from the urgencies of poverty and powerlessness—that should be their own work; that is domestic justice. And for that there is no time constraint; the work goes on and on. At any given moment, leftists (and everyone else) are simply engaged.

I propose that we think about domestic distributive justice much as we think about self-determination and the politics of liberation. Each collective self must determine itself by itself; each liberation is of and by a particular group of people. The process is reiterative. Some selves may imitate earlier determinations, or they may choose to determine themselves by way of contrast. But whatever they do, they must do it by themselves. Similarly, as the old left maxim says, "The liberation of the working class must be the work of the working class itself." Or, again, national liberation must be the work of each oppressed or subordinate nation. Even when the project of liberation receives support from around the world, from dissident citizens of the oppressor states, for example, the militants of national liberation do not want external supporters to determine what liberation means for their nation. Only its own people can rightly do that. Similarly, the distribution of social goods must be decided by the men and women who make, value, and distribute the goods. They must figure out for themselves what justice requires. Can they get it wrong? Well, "they" is ambiguous. Some of them can certainly get it wrong; many of them can get it wrong some of the time; but I doubt that all of them can get it wrong all the time.

How does it happen that some of them get it wrong? Two ways are centrally important. The first failure of domestic justice occurs when the shared understandings on which distribution is based are not in fact as widely shared as local elites pretend. Not so long ago, for example, elite groups defended slavery by claiming that the slaves accepted their condition and loved their masters; slavery was a traditional and benevolent institution. More recently, similar groups have defended the subordination of women by claiming that women are themselves committed to the prevailing gender ideology and that they accept the distribution of work, wages, and respect that follow from it. I suppose there were individual slaves and women who fit these descriptions, but not many. In a world of radically unequal power, the forms of denial and resistance may be devious, almost invisible, but they are real nonetheless.

Because resistance is so hard to recognize, some leftist critics of domestic distributions repeat the claims of the elites, although they assign a different significance to them. They argue that oppressed men and women don't know they are oppressed because they have been taken in by the ideology of their oppressors; they are victims of false consciousness. By contrast, these critics have a true understanding of the oppression, they hold the correct ideological position, and they know the necessary political response. They are often right, I think, about the existence of injustice and the need for a political response. But they commonly misjudge the men and women on whose behalf they claim to be speaking, and they fail to grasp the kind of response these people must make if justice is to be their own work. As I said earlier, the theory of false consciousness points toward a vanguard politics that is likely to lead to a grossly unequal distribution of political power.

Again: the work of liberation must be the work of the men and women who need to be liberated. It follows that the definition of liberation should be their own. Other people can help them—they will often need help—but it must not be the others who determine their future. Other people can criticize their work and urge them to adopt a different view of a liberated life, but this must be criticism only; it must never turn into domination. There is no single authoritative account of how a liberation struggle should go or what a liberated life looks like.

The second failure of domestic justice occurs when one much-valued social good is used to usurp other goods without regard to the meaning of the other goods. State power in the former Soviet Union dominated the distribution of education, medical care, and housing. Communist Party membership, which ostensibly was an indication only of ideological commitment and political work, was a necessary and sufficient criterion for professional advance. Similarly, in many Western countries, market success and the accumulation of money dominate the distribution of social goods that are ostensibly not for sale—including political office and criminal justice. In the Islamic republic of Iran, religious commitments that are said to bring eternal life also bring political power and legal authority in this life.

These distortions of distributive justice can be resisted only by people with an interest in and an understanding of the usurped goods. Teachers and students defend the autonomy of schools; doctors, nurses, and patients insist on the integrity of medical practice; believers argue for the independence of religious institutions from state control; ordinary citizens argue for the independence of state institutions from religious control; citizens call for a welfare system whose fairness they can recognize and whose priorities they accept, or for an electoral system in which their votes count. Leftists ought to support all these efforts. These are the everyday battles through which justice is pursued, and they are local battles, necessarily fought by particular people in particular times and places. We watch how they go in other countries and learn from the others—or not.

In these battles, the state is both an object and an instrument. It is an object in that we argue about how political power and office are rightly distributed; these two are social goods like any others. But the state is also an instrument of distribution, providing welfare, guaranteeing impartial justice and free elections, determining what money can and cannot buy and what limits should be set to the influence of powerful men and women. Imagine that these instrumental uses of state power are democratically determined. They will be shaped and reshaped by popular opinion, by the local version of common sense and conventional belief, by historical memory, and by ideological debate. The distributions that result may be legitimate even if some comprehensive theory declares them wrong. And even if they are both legitimate and right (all social goods are distributed in accordance with their meaning to the men and women who make and distribute them), the results will never be final. Difference and disagreement will work their way, and the distributive arguments will be renewed again and again. Leftists committed to greater equality in this or that distribution will have to join these arguments.

Relief and repair, the primary forms of global justice, are also never finished, but we can imagine at least a rough agreement on the principles that guide them. We can imagine a world in which all existing states are capable of self-help, so that mutual aid and reparative justice are only intermittently and occasionally required— and forthcoming whenever they are required. The imagining is easy, but we are still very far from that world, very far from the global justice that people need *right now*. But even if that world is far away, men and women who are free from the urgencies of poverty and powerlessness are already engaged in the pursuit of domestic justice and in the unending arguments about social goods and values that it requires. One way of expressing the political project I am advocating here is to say that everyone should have the justice they need *right now* so that they can pursue the justice they will never finally have.

SIX

World Government and the Politics of Pretending

World government is mostly a leftist utopia, a dream about a time to come. But in some of its possible versions, it is a nightmare. A global tyranny—Immanuel Kant's "universal monarchy," which would also be, he writes, a "soulless despotism"—is undoubtedly one form of world government, perhaps the most likely form.[1] A global state might well take shape in the same way particular states took shape in early modern Europe, beginning as an absolutist regime. Tyrannical rule anywhere is nightmarish, but the great advantage of the society of sovereign states is that at any given moment there are alternatives to tyranny: other regimes, some of which might even have souls. There are countries that can provide refuge for political exiles and countries that are models or approximations of liberal and democratic rule. Books banned in one place can be published in another. The great advantage of today's world order is its pluralism; it is only very late at night that I think about its replacement by a single all-encompassing state. Still, even pluralism requires some governing arrangement, some set of relatively stable practices and decision-making processes, and it is certainly possible to imagine a better-governed world than the one we have. What might that require?

I will begin with an unconventional suggestion, which I have intimated in earlier chapters. A better-governed world requires first the completion of state-building and boundary drawing. The people who talk about transcending the state system are mostly those living in securely established states with recognized borders. People without states (Palestinians, Kurds, and Tibetans, for example), and those living in predatory states or in failed states that cannot defend their borders or populations against sectarian militias and mercenary adventurers—none of these people are interested in political transcendence or world government. They have a different dream. They want a state of their own, a decent and competent state capable of providing the routine benefits of sovereignty: physical protection, economic management, welfare, and education. The worst conflicts in the world today, the most extensive human suffering, derive from statelessness and state failure.

This seems to me an obvious point, yet many people on the left are, or claim to be, hostile to the state, especially to the nation-state, which is the most common state formation in the world today. They indict the nation-state for its parochialism, its chauvinism, and the nationalist furies it sometimes unleashes. Early in the history of the left, this was a genuinely universalist argument. Rosa Luxemburg, for example, wrote with equal derision about Poles, Ukrainians, Lithuanians, Czechs, Yugoslavs, Jews, and "ten new nations of the Caucasus." She saw only "rotting corpses [that] climb up out of hundred year old graves . . . [and] feel a passionate urge to form states."[2] More recently, however, leftists have been (rightly) sympathetic to national liberation and the formation of new states in India, Indonesia, Sri Lanka, Vietnam, Algeria, Ghana, Rhodesia, Angola, Bangladesh, and many other places; and today

we are (rightly again) sympathetic to Palestinian national liberation. We are mostly enthusiastic (when we should be wary) about
populist nationalism in Venezuela, Bolivia, and other Latin American countries. We provided strong (and justified) support for the
Greek assertion of national interest against the EU and its bankers.
We welcomed (along with everybody else) the Arab Spring and the
efforts in countries like Egypt and Tunisia to transform, but definitely not to transcend, the existing nation-states.

All these are exceptions to the general rule of leftist hostility to
the nation-state. What is curious here is that the exceptions to the
rule far outnumber its applications. The crucial application is to
Jewish statehood in Israel: across much of the left, opposition to Zi-
onism determines the correct ideological position on the national
question. A few other cases seem to fall under the general rule: a
widespread indifference on the left to Kurdish national liberation
is one example; another is the readiness of many leftists to oppose
local nationalists in Georgia and Ukraine and to make apologies for
Russian imperialism.[3]

Leftists are also opposed to nationalism at home, to all the na-
tive-born bigots and anti-immigrant politicians, but that hostility
fits neatly (in the United States and elsewhere) with the default
position. The prevailing view of nationalism abroad seems to be
driven by a kind of ideological fury at the state of Israel and by
the demand that it be replaced by a bi-national or, better, post-
national "state of all its citizens"—a state identified with none of
them.[4] I won't attempt to explain the fury; the long history of left
anti-Semitism, "the socialism of fools," is only part of the explanation.[5] Opposition to Israeli occupation of the West Bank and Gaza
accounts for much of the support for an anti-only-Israel politics,
but it doesn't explain the origin of this politics or its singular focus.
Nor is there any reason to believe that the end of the occupation
and the establishment of a Palestinian state alongside Israel (which

is a legitimate aim of the international left) would bring an acceptance of Israeli legitimacy by those who now deny it.

Still, there are men and women on the left with an entirely different position, more like the one I mean to defend here: a state for all the people who need one—which means for everyone, including the Jews.

Helping people in failed states may require forms of military intervention that violate the principle of state sovereignty. But the long-term goal of these interventions is to establish or strengthen sovereignty; that's what state-building means. Even if no one knows how to build states in places where centralized power has collapsed, where warlords rule or rival religious sects massacre each other's members, the project that the intervening forces have to set themselves, once the killing has been stopped, is to create some legitimate local authority. Whatever the difficulties, they must aim at an effective state, with a government sufficiently popular to govern without excessive coercion. This is a minimal goal, certainly not a transcendent one, but it is practical and necessary.

I don't imagine universal peace following from the completion of the state system, but local peace—here and here; peace in pieces. The creation of new states and decent states is genuinely leftist work. We can think of it as the defense of human rights, which are radically at risk in the absence of effective government. In the world as we know it, and as we are likely to know it for years to come, a decent state is the best agency for the protection of human rights. NGOs like Human Rights Watch and Amnesty International report on the chronic misbehavior of states and hope for internal correction, but they can't themselves protect the people whose rights are being violated. They are working for regime change (although they may be unwilling to acknowledge it), but the regimes they hope to change are, and can only be, state regimes.

We can also think of the work of completion, the necessary step toward a better-governed world, as a redistribution of resources, since only wealthier and more powerful states can bear the costs of state-building. Since these states are often former imperial or colonial powers, the costs they must bear are not entirely philanthropic. They are often morally obligatory; they follow from the reparative justice I described in the last chapter. When genuinely independent states, committed to the safety and security of their people, are created with outside help, a debt is usually being paid. State-building is the opposite of imperialism and colonialism: it is a repudiation of both. A completed state system would therefore be a more just international society.

A possible model for this work of completion is John Locke's argument for religious toleration. The men and women who yearn for independence and effective government are like the seventeenth-century dissident Protestants who yearned for religious freedom and political protection. "The establishment of this one thing," Locke wrote in his *Letter Concerning Toleration*, "would take away all ground of complaints and tumults on account of conscience."[6] The "one thing" for Locke was religious toleration—a free church for every believer. The one thing today is a decent and competent state for every subject and citizen. And the ground of complaints and tumults today is the absence of national independence and physical safety. Take away this ground—that is, provide all the world's peoples with independence (or some functional equivalent) and security—and the world would be a more peaceful place. Again, this seems an obvious point.

Locke goes on: "There is only one thing which gathers people into seditious commotions, and that is oppression."[7] National oppression has the same "gathering" effects as religious oppression, but now we have to add that anarchy and lawlessness, the absence of effective government, civil war, or, worse, Hobbes's "war of all against all"—these can be as oppressive as a persecuting orthodoxy or a political tyranny, even if they don't have the same gathering effects and even if the "commotions" aren't seditious, as perhaps they should be. Peace will come when conscience is quiet, when national aspirations are accommodated, and when people feel that everyday life is reasonably secure.

But the quiet conscience is much easier to imagine than the satisfied nation or the secure population. We have some experience of consciences at peace; liberal states have made Lockeian toleration an everyday reality, with results very close to what Locke predicted. Disagreement and conflict persist insofar as religion continues to be a serious concern of (some) liberal citizens, but the sorts of tumult that roiled the seventeenth century have been surpassed wherever states have given up religious persecution and achieved some measure of separation between religion and politics.

Would a similar result follow if every form of national subjugation and state breakdown were overcome? This second political transformation cannot be made effective in the same way as the first. Any number of religious groups can be tolerated on the same territory, but each people needs a territory of its own if it is to achieve political autonomy or sovereignty within secure boundaries. Self-determination, unlike religious freedom, requires a physical space and a monopoly on the use of force within that space. But this space, with its boundaries clearly marked, is not instantly available or naturally (or divinely) assigned to particular groups of people. It has to be appropriated in one way or another, and the appropriation will often be contested—not only by imperial powers but also by other nations looking out for their citizens' security. So complaint and tumult don't end; one nation's freedom is often another nation's oppression.

All this might account for leftist hostility to the nation-state if this hostility were in fact consistent. But it isn't, and what is more important, it shouldn't be. The men and women caught up in national conflicts are not usually led to forgo the hope of statehood and sovereignty, and these are people to whom the left should be responsive. Nor are the liberation struggles, the great power interventions, the contention of rival militias and feuding sects, and all the civil wars necessarily endless and endlessly destructive. There are useful historical examples of vindicated claims to independence and security. The separation of Norway and Sweden and of the Czech Republic and Slovakia are useful examples of the two-state solution; the breakup of the Soviet Union, of the many-state solution; the creation of East Timor and Kosovo, of successful secessions (with outside help). Another example is the restored unity of Nigeria after its civil war. We can, moreover, imagine the reconstruction of failed states, even if successful cases are hard to find. Independence and security do bring, or would bring, if only locally, something like the peace that the Lockeian argument promises.

Good borders make good neighbors.[8] Secession, partition, and liberation, the repression of private militias and the preservation of political unions—these processes, all aimed at statehood and security, point the way toward a kind of global settlement.

The way itself is bloody enough, and I acknowledge that there are cases where people from different nations are so closely entangled on the same piece of territory that a good border is inconceivable. Then the hope is for some version of federalism or autonomy and a central government strong enough to keep the peace. In one way or another, the completion of the state system is a reform worth pursuing. National liberation movements and governments-in-the-making will pursue it, but other states should pursue it, too, helping from the outside or sometimes intervening directly to stop destructive civil wars or massacres. The goal is a world of states with relatively secure borders, a world from which no sizable group of people is excluded. Is this a utopian program? Yes, in the sense that such a world does not exist. No, in the sense that the achievement of statehood and security by one set of peoples after another is actually happening. That the process is uneven, that it is sometimes violent, that it produces anomalies along the way (nations without states, states with more than one nation): none of these is sufficient reason to back away from it.

After Sovereignty

I want to add immediately that the completion of the state system is not any kind of historical endpoint. There is no end of history. Precisely because of the difficulties along the way to completion, further processes are set in motion, and these are not similarly constrained by the idea of sovereignty. The first such process is decentralization within states. Sensible governments often try to secure peace and stability, and hold off secessionist movements, by granting autonomy to some regionally centered ethnic group. But political prudence isn't the only reason to defend decentralization; it is also a way to open new room for cultural expression and democratic self-government.

Partial devolutions of sovereignty may meet the needs of ethnic or religious minorities that have maintained some territorial integrity; they are not yet a dispersed population but are no longer so differentiated from the bulk of their fellow citizens as to require (or want) full independence. Some degree of autonomy is sufficient for their purposes, at least as most of them define their purposes. There are sometimes more radical groups that demand secession and state sovereignty, but the frequency with which these groups resort to terrorism is an index of their lack of popular support. The devolution of sovereignty, rather than its entire appropriation, suffices in these cases for the defense of group identity and physical security. Or, better, we can plausibly imagine that it would suffice. The test of its sufficiency is more likely to come in old and established states than in new ones—autonomy for the Welsh, Quebeckers,

Catalans, or Basques, for example. The hard work of state-building makes new political elites suspicious of decentralization, even when it would serve them well; they are unwilling to share the power they have so recently acquired. The case of Iraqi Kurdistan provides a useful example, both of the suspicion among the new rulers in Baghdad and of autonomy's obvious usefulness. Older elites are more likely to surrender some of their power in order to hold the rest with less trouble.

The second, more important and riskier process that follows from the completion of the state system is the creation of new federations and economic and political unions among sovereign states. The European Union is the obvious example, and there is much to learn from its vicissitudes and also from its triumphs. The most important lessons are that an economic union is problematic if it is not accompanied by and governed by a strong and democratic political union and that the construction of a political union is enormously difficult because of preexisting national loyalties. The EU features a neo-liberal economy without a social-democratic government, and therefore it has failed to do justice to its weakest member states, such as Greece, and it has also failed to do justice to its weakest individual members, the large number of men and women left behind by the free movement of capital, commodities, and workers. Justice was once an issue dealt with through domestic politics; that politics has now been partially taken over by the EU and replaced by administration. But the administration, for all its famous regulations, doesn't govern the neo-liberal economy so much as accommodate it.

The old nation-states survive within the EU, and if they aren't allowed to impose some constraints on free movement or establish some protection against its adverse effects, their resentful citizens will produce a nationalist backlash—first seen in the 2016 British vote to leave the EU. As I write, populist, nationalist, and anti-European movements are gaining strength in many countries (and the election of Donald Trump in the United States has given them a transatlantic warrant). Leftists must look for some way to accommodate national feelings and defeat nationalist zealotry. It might help to think of organizations like the EU in internationalist rather than cosmopolitan terms. The difference is important. Internationalism assumes the existence of nations and works to create obligations and solidarities across national boundaries. By contrast, cosmopolitanism is a globalist ideology; it aims to abolish boundaries, which in the contemporary world is almost certainly a step too far.

There is another way to express the immediate leftist worry about unions like the EU. The nation-state is still the only political space within which the left has been able to win political victories. It is the home of social-democracy and welfare. Indeed, the nation-state and the welfare state go together—and the more homogeneous the nation-state, the stronger its welfare system. Nonetheless, it seems to me that leftists should be actively trying to expand the political space within which we can work effectively. Michael Rustin, writing in 1985, described "the attractions of political work in an expanded European dimension." He saw such work as an opportunity for socialists, organizing across political boundaries, to forge links equal to the "much more powerful links" that already exist between national corporations and governments.[9] Too many socialist leaders, beguiled by neo-liberal economic theory, abandoned this ambition, and partly for that reason the left hasn't been able to create those new links or realize the economic promise of expansion: that activity across wider political spaces would make more resources available for redistribution. That was the original hope of left-wing supporters of the European Union, and it should be remembered when leftists rally to defend the EU against right-wing populists and nationalists.

Nor should we forget the great achievement of the EU: the transformation of Europe from a zone of war to a zone of peace. This is an important (though incomplete) transcendence of both the limits and the dangers of sovereignty. It is a transcendence of the limits in that the union makes for greater power and a stronger and therefore safer position in the global economy and the arenas of international politics. It is a transcendence of the dangers insofar as the government of the union provides mechanisms for making difficult decisions and dealing with persistent interstate conflicts. Today these mechanisms are neither democratic nor secure; nor is it clear what loyalty the EU commands from its diverse citizenry— above all, from its richest and poorest members, who have different reasons for opting out. But union and alliance now stand as possible and hopeful moves beyond sovereign statehood. We just have to find the right distance: not too far beyond.

I don't want to forget the failures of the United Arab Republic and the East African economic union in the 1970s and the weakness today of regional associations like the African Union and the Arab League—which suggest that statehood still has the primary claim on most of the world's peoples. And I don't want to deny that the completion of the state system has caused and will cause significant disintegration, as we saw in the collapse of the Soviet Union. Statehood for Tibet and full recognition of the independence of Taiwan, both presently impossible but necessary features of my project, suggest further disintegration. For that very reason, it is important to argue that as soon as the state system is completed and the promise of disintegration is fulfilled, a new process of alliance and unification should begin.

This is in fact the European story. The post–World War II settlement, which guaranteed the independence of all the states west of the Soviet bloc and established secure boundaries for them, made European unification a real possibility. Unification is not on the historical agenda for subjugated peoples and insecure or failed states. Only lines firmly drawn on the map can be transformed by commerce, communication, and politics into dotted lines. Broken boundaries, inhabited on either side by mercenaries and militias, have to be fixed before they can be safely transcended.

If, therefore, we are interested in one or another version of African unification (for example), the place to begin is with an effective state system. As Europe needed a definitive postwar settlement, so Africa needs a definitive post-colonial settlement. That may require the partition of some existing states (however bloody, as in Sudan), even though African sentiment right now strongly opposes partition. Or it may require the consolidation of states as they are, through internal political processes if possible or else with outside help. But the state system won't be transcended so long as most Africans are still seeking the benefits it is supposed to provide—law and order above all, maintained by a police force whose coercive power is recognized as legitimate.

While we wait for processes of unification to develop and mature, and as we work to advance them, there is another internationalist project that leftists and others should pursue: the creation, through multilateral treaties, of arrangements and regulations that advance such critically important goals as climate control, nuclear disarmament, and global public health. There is a fairly common left argument that sovereign statehood stands in the way of all such arrangements. Jonathan Schell, in *The Fate of the Earth*, argues that "national sovereignty" brings us face-to-face with the "peril of extinction." Anthony Barnett, at the end of a brilliant polemic against Margaret Thatcher's Falklands War, repeats the warning: "So long as the institutions and passions of nationalist sovereignty retain their domination, in Britain as elsewhere, the world will continue to be ruled by those who are likely to ensure its destruction."[10]

This argument is perfectly compatible with the defense of national liberation in countries like Algeria, since it is aimed chiefly at the sovereignty of the great powers. Still, we had better hope it isn't right, for only sovereign states can enter into self-limiting unions like the EU or sign treaties like the Non-Proliferation Treaty. The path to disarmament and climate control goes through the sovereign state, especially through the most powerful sovereign states, because that's where social movements with global ambitions get started. That's where the internationalist left has to begin its effort to set limits on sovereignty.

I urged the importance of limits while discussing hegemony in chapter 4; the argument also applies to sovereignty, which can be thought of as a form of local hegemony. Both the hegemon and the sovereign are capable of self-limitation, but they are most likely to accept the limits necessary for a better world order if they are pressed by a militant left. But the militant left must also be an intelligent left, whose members understand that although sovereign states can make war, sometimes foolishly and criminally (as in the Falklands—or in Iraq), they can also make peace. No other political agent now standing can do that.

Pretending

In the absence of world government, what kinds of governmental arrangements can there be, or should there be, among sovereign states? What can we do at the global level? What we already do is not negligible, although it is less than it appears to be—and much less than many people pretend it is. We have a global constitution, the UN Charter; a global bill of rights, the 1948 Universal Declaration of Human Rights; a global parliament, the General Assembly; a global executive committee, the Security Council; a global judiciary, the World Court and the International Criminal Court (ICC); a global banking system, the International Monetary Fund (IMF) and the World Bank; a global agency to regulate trade, the

World Trade Organization (WTO); and a global agency to protect workers' rights, the International Labor Organization (ILO). But neither the constitution nor the bill of rights has ever been enforced; parliamentary decisions are merely advisory; the executive committee is usually deadlocked; the courts cannot compete with state legal systems; neither the international banks nor the trade organization played a significant positive role during the recent global recession; and almost no one has even heard of the ILO.

Let's look more carefully at the three most important of these global institutions: the Security Council, the courts, and the IMF, and ask what they are in fact and what they might be.

The Security Council. The Security Council is the executive arm of the United Nations, which is itself nothing more than a simulacrum of world government. The council is not an effective organization. The veto power of its five permanent members is commonly seen as the major cause of paralysis. But there is another reason for inaction, less discussed but probably more important in the long run. Each member of the council thinks only in terms of its own national interests. There is no overriding sense, or even an underlying sense, of being responsible for the way the world goes. The world is not a political unit for which anybody feels responsible in the way (some) political elites in domestic societies feel responsible for the fate of their country and the well-being of its citizens. In democratic states, those elites can, in principle at least, be forced to act responsibly or else be removed from office. Nothing like that is possible in international society or at the United Nations. Confronted with a human disaster in Rwanda or Darfur, council members take their stands based on a calculation of their parochial interests. It matters very little what these stands mean for the people most at risk, who have no power and are regarded more as victims than as fellow citizens of a global community. Until they are seen as fellow citizens, the Security Council won't be an effective agent on their behalf, which is why, right now, people at risk need a state of their own.

Everyone knows that the Security Council cannot prevent wars, fight them, or end them. The usual leftist demand to take this or that issue (the 9/11 attack is my standard example) to the council is an unacknowledged demand that nothing be done. This is the politics of pretending. It works pretty well. Bringing a crisis to the United Nations is a way of pretending to act while closing one's eyes and turning one's back. The political leaders (and the citizens, too) of states strong enough to intervene can call for UN intervention, do nothing themselves, and escape responsibility for the disasters that follow.

It is possible to imagine a council that could act, at least in dire emergencies, to rescue people at risk, perhaps with a standing force whose soldiers would not have to be recruited, from reluctant states, in the midst of a crisis. The UN commander in Rwanda in 1994 thought that he could stop the killing if the five thousand soldiers at his disposal were reinforced, but the Security Council (partly because of US opposition) couldn't agree to authorize him to act.[11] A high-tech army on the US model isn't needed, just something much less—hence also something much less than the army of a global state. A few UN successes in places like Rwanda and Darfur would transform its image. But success would require a sense of responsibility among the great powers, as well as smaller states, that is radically absent today. And it would require some way of giving a political voice to people at risk in whatever part of the world.

Right now, successful military intervention is the work of states that find it in their interest to stop mass murder or terror in nearby countries, as in the examples I discussed in chapter 3. Or perhaps it is the work of morally embarrassed states or coalitions of states, like NATO in Kosovo after the humiliation of failing to protect the people of Srebenica. These interventions had to be unilateral,

since there was no chance of UN approval, but the subsequent political reconstruction (state-building) could have been conducted
under UN-authorized mandates or trusteeships. The Cambodian
elections of 1993, organized directly by UN officials, might serve
as a model for reconstructions to come. If there are some successes,
the idea of trusteeship or direct UN engagement might then be
extended backward to the interventions themselves.

The International Courts. International courts can resolve disputes
only when the states involved want them resolved. The 2009 case
of the International Criminal Court and the president of Sudan
tells us a great deal about the character of global justice today—
and about its unacknowledged dangers.[12] The court's indictment
of Omar al-Bashir for crimes against humanity in Darfur may one
day be recognized as a critical precedent in the development of an
international judicial system and the defense of human rights. In
2009, however, the ICC was acting as the judicial arm of a world
government that did not exist—another example of pretending.
Its decisions could not be enforced, and when those decisions put
people at risk, the court could not protect them. When al-Bashir
expelled aid organizations from Sudan, he was retaliating against
Darfurians for the ICC's action against him; he was deliberately
provoking a humanitarian crisis or, more accurately, intensifying the
crisis that already existed. And there was nothing the court could
do—and nothing any other agency of global government could do
in its name. I know the value that even a costly precedent might
have in the future, but the immediate consequences were severe.
Pretending that an effective system of global justice exists when it
doesn't seems to me morally and politically irresponsible.

Still, again, it is possible to imagine an international court that
acts only in concert with a military intervention authorized by
the United Nations—in conditions where it could secure indicted
criminals and protect other people from any political retaliation

the indictment might bring. The court that dealt with the former Yugoslavia perhaps provides a useful if limited example. There can be no pretense that this court was the judicial arm of a fully functioning world government. But successful prosecutions like those in The Hague do move the world toward something like a remedial system of global justice. The most immediate necessity is to supplement the justice done in (relatively) decent and competent states with an internationally authorized form of judicial action for states that have failed or collapsed.

The IMF and the World Bank. Until the Great Recession of 2008, global economic management might have been considered more of a success story than global political management. Certainly, there were economists at the International Monetary Fund and World Bank who had some sense of responsibility for the well-being of all the inhabitants of the globe. But this sense was shaped by a particular ideology, neo-liberalism, or the "Washington consensus," and not by responsiveness to the felt needs or aspirations of those inhabitants. Critics would say that this ideology reflected the interests of a small group of wealthy nations—but if so, these nations seem to have been wrong about their interests. The policies promoted by the IMF stimulated global economic growth for a time, but it has been apparent at least since the Asian financial crisis of 1998 that they also contributed to instability by producing radical inequalities within many countries—between the center and the periphery, between urban and rural areas, between the technical elite and workers with lesser skills. We have watched the growing separation between the very well-off and the desperately poor. Stable growth requires that more and more people participate as producers and consumers in the global economy —and that requires in turn a more egalitarian global society.

In democratic states, there is a remedy for gross inequality. Angry men and women organize social movements, trade unions, and political parties to challenge the economic hierarchy, regulate the market, and redistribute the wealth. Social-democracy reshapes laissez-faire capitalism. But this happens, as I have argued, only in domestic societies, not yet in international society (and not yet in the EU either). Cosmopolitan leftists, who imagine that declining sovereignty and open borders will lead to a more egalitarian world, are engaged in yet another version of the politics of pretending. Right now, campaigns against inequality take place only in the sovereign state, and it is only there that we see the negotiations, compromises, and new social arrangements that those campaigns make possible. Domestic political leaders and economic managers act for and in response to organized popular constituencies. But the IMF is not subject to the approval of any organized popular constituency. Even if its managers feel responsible for global well-being, their responsibility is not politically enforced or enforceable. They do not answer to the people for whom they are responsible.

I don't see any ready or easy way to make them answerable. That would require, again, leftist politics in some kind of global space that is as yet undiscovered. Right now, only political work within particular states, and probably only particular wealthy states, can force changes in the policies of the IMF, the World Bank, and the WTO. Elected leaders in the United States, Japan, the EU, and a few other places can pressure the global economic bureaucrats. But they will do this only in response to demands from men and women at home. The way to a social-democratic IMF and to greater global equality lies through state politics—and that's also the way to disarmament and climate control. We can hope for cooperation across state boundaries in pursuit of greater equality (by international trade unions, for example, or by new social movements); there is, after all, extensive cooperation among corporate elites in shaping the policies that produce the inequality we live with today. But elites function easily in international society, whereas the space for mass action has yet to be found.

A Provisional Left Program

Here, then, is a provisional left program, not for world government but for better government in the world. The first step: providing all the world's people with a decent and competent state. I know that isn't an easy thing to do, but it is possible, gradually, incrementally, here and here. What is most important is that the value of statehood be recognized. There is too much loose talk about transcending the state system, when the greatest need of the world's poorest and most oppressed people is full participation in that system.

As statehood is achieved and stabilized, it also needs to be complicated by devolution and alliance. Nurturing the second of these is probably the more important next step to take. Economic and political cooperation across borders can greatly enhance the benefits of sovereignty, and it can also provide intimations of transcendence and global government. The early redistribution of resources within the EU, for example, suggests the kind of work that could be done by a social-democratic IMF. Similarly, the coordination of military activity by EU states—the formation of a rapid deployment force, for example (if it were ever rapidly deployed)—could provide a model for a future UN Security Council.

Third, we must aim to reinforce international institutions—the Security Council, the ICC, the IMF, and others—that can provide background regulation, act effectively in emergencies, and fill the gaps opened up by state failure or incapacity. I don't think they should try to do more than that—but just that would be an enormous benefit.

People living in decent and competent states don't need a global state or an everyday world government. But they need something else, something I have mentioned several times in this book but have barely discussed. They need, all of us already need, a global civil society. This is where space might be found for politics across borders. This is where groups like Human Rights Watch and Amnesty International, groups that are born, so to speak, at home, can agitate for human rights abroad. This is where environmental issues can be raised and states can be pressed to respond to dangers that do not respect boundaries. This is where unions that call themselves international can become international in fact and express solidarity with unorganized and underpaid workers around the world. And this is where a new generation of activists might find a voice.

Exactly how politics would work in a developed transnational civil society we don't know. What kinds of mobilization might be possible? What kinds of debate and deliberation? There are plenty of reasons to be skeptical and worried; this isn't a familiar political space, and it may not be a friendly one. But if we hope for a decent global politics after statehood—and right now, too—we need an active and open civil society where people speaking different languages, with different political loyalties, recruited from all over, can engage with each other. Engagements will begin at home, but they have to find their way beyond the boundaries of the state. This is the fourth step toward better global government.

So this is the full program: first, gradual completion of the state system to provide security for citizens; second, a slow process of political alliance among states to create wider and wider zones of peace; third, the improvement of existing international institutions; and fourth, the creation of a space for the political engagement of individual men and women, without regard to their citizenship. I won't pretend that this is a revolutionary program. Each of its parts can only be approached incrementally. Indeed, a historian friend told me that it sounded like a very old-fashioned program— something like the vision of global order that inspired liberals and leftists in the aftermath of World War II. Those were years of optimism, and in this darker time, it may help to recall what we once hoped to achieve.

SEVEN

The Left and Religion

The Case of Islam

In the nearly four decades since the Iranian revolution, I have watched my fellow leftists struggle to understand or avoid understanding the revival of religion in what is now called a post-secular age. Long ago we all accepted the truth of Max Weber's "disenchantment of the world"—the belief that the triumph of science and reason was a necessary feature of modernity. We thought it certain that one or another version of secularism would emerge triumphant: the neutral state, the retreat of religion to the private sphere, universal toleration. Since we believed that religious faith was slowly disappearing, or at least that the remaining faithful were disengaging from political life, we stopped worrying about religion. And so we forgot, as Nick Cohen has written, "what the men and women of the Enlightenment knew. All faiths in their extreme form carry the possibility of tyranny."[1]

Now, every major world religion is experiencing a significant revival, and revived religion, contrary to what we once believed, isn't an opiate; it is a very strong stimulant. But the religious stimulant isn't everywhere the same. Since the late 1970s, and particularly in the past decade, it has worked most powerfully in the Islamic world. From Pakistan to Nigeria and in parts of Europe, Islam today inspires small but significant numbers of men and women to join organizations that resemble the old International Brigades and to kill and die for religious reasons. The religious revival in general and Islamism in particular have created a kind of testing moment for the left: Can we recognize and resist the possibility of tyranny?

Some of us are trying to meet the test; many of us are actively failing it. One reason for the failure of many leftists to acknowledge and confront Islamist zealotry is the fear of being called Islamophobic. Certainly, leftists everywhere must stand against nationalist and populist campaigns targeting Muslim immigrants. The resurgent right in Europe and now in the United States requires an unyielding left opposition. But that can't be a reason for giving up the classic left-wing struggle against religious zeal, which has been going on since the Enlightenment. As in many other cases, we have to fight on two fronts at once.

There are other equally important explanations for the reluctance of many leftists to fight on the anti-zealot front. For all those who believe "The enemy of my enemy is my friend," leftist anti-Americanism motivates an apologetic or defensive response to Islamism. The left's disbelief in the power of faith produces a search for materialist accounts of religious zeal: poverty, oppression, and imperialism must be the root causes of zeal—and so they should be the sole objects of left opposition. A radical version of cultural relativism further undercuts any strong critique of religious tyranny. Consequently, many leftists haven't been willing to consider the very good reasons for criticizing and actively opposing today's zealots.

There is no left collective, no singular left view of religion, but the people I will discuss in this chapter constitute a significant force

on the left, a diverse force but one that is ideologically connected—
and opposed by other forces to which I am more sympathetic. I
will provide many examples because the controversies are newer
and stranger than any I have considered in previous chapters. Indeed, religion has hardly figured at all in left debates about foreign policy—from the sympathetic response of American radicals
to Greek rebels in the 1820s (when Orthodox religion might have
been something to worry about) right up to the arguments about
Iraq in 2003 (when Sunni and Shi'ite sectarianism was certainly
something to worry about). Today, religion should be at the center
of our political consciousness.

I myself live with a general fear of every form of religious militancy. I am afraid of Hindutva zealots in India, messianic Zionists
in Israel, and rampaging Buddhist monks in Myanmar. But I am
most afraid of Islamists, not because I have any prejudicial feelings
about Islam or any lack of admiration for its cultural achievements,
but because the Islamic world at this moment (not always, not forever) is especially feverish and fervent.

Is this an anti-Muslim position? Does it grow out of hostility
and hatred? Consider a rough analogy (all analogies are rough).
If I say that Christianity in the eleventh and twelfth centuries was
a crusading religion, and that in those years it was dangerous to
Jews and Muslims, who were rightly fearful, would that make me
anti-Christian? I know that crusading fervor isn't essential to the
Christian religion; it is historically contingent, and the crusading
moment in Christian history came and, after two hundred years or
so, went. Saladin, sultan and commander, helped bring it to an end,
but it would have ended on its own. Many contemporary Christians opposed the Crusades; today we would call those Christians
moderates. Nor were most contemporary Christians interested in
crusading warfare; they listened to sermons urging them to march
to Jerusalem and then went home to supper. Still, for many years

many of the physical, material, and intellectual resources of Christendom were focused on the Crusades.

In *Islamophobia and the Politics of Empire*, Deepa Kumar describes the Christian Crusades as the first example of Islamophobia in the West.[2] Kumar's first book was a strongly pro-labor study of the 1997 UPS workers' strike. More ambitious now, she provides a world-historical account of the irrational fear of Islam, beginning with the crusaders. So far as I can tell, none of the book's enthusiastic reviewers have accused Kumar of being hostile to Christianity. The case could be made for hostility or at least for partisanship: although she correctly refers to the aim of the Crusades as the "reconquest" of the Holy Land, she barely mentions the previous Muslim conquest. Still, it probably makes sense to include the crusaders in the long list of Islamophobes—and the even longer list of Judeophobes. They were fierce and frightening religious extremists, and that assertion is not anti-Christian.

Similar things can (and should) be said about Islamists today—even though jihadi violence is not required by Islamic theology, even though there are many Muslim moderates who oppose religious violence, and even though most Muslims are quite happy to leave infidels and heretics to their otherworldly fate. I know that there is a "jihad of the soul" in addition to the "jihad of the sword," and that Muhammad famously declared the first of these to be the greater jihad. And I recognize that the Islamic world is not monolithic. Reading the daily newspaper, anyone can see that even Islamist zealotry is not all of a piece. Al Qaeda, the Taliban, the Islamic State of Iraq and Syria (ISIS), Hamas, and Boko Haram, to take just a few leading examples, are not the same; there may well be significant theological disagreements among them. I should note, also, that many millions of Muslims in Indonesia and India seem relatively untouched by the current zealotry, although Jemaah Islamiyah, a Southeast Asian Islamist network, has followers in Indonesia and has been credited, if that's the right word, with terrorist attacks against infidels there.

Despite these qualifications, the jihad of the sword is very strong today, and it is frightening to unbelievers, heretics, secular liberals, social-democrats, and liberated women in much of the Muslim world. This fear is entirely rational. It is equally rational to fear all the other religious zealots, but some men and women on the left seem to find it harder to fear the Islamists. Acknowledging the causal power of religious faith remains a general problem; Islamism today is a very specific problem.

Islamophobia

Many leftists are less afraid of Islamists than of Islamophobia. This is an odd position given what's happening every day in the Muslim world, but it makes considerable sense in western Europe and America, where Muslims are recent immigrants, the objects of discrimination, demagogic attack, police surveillance, and sometimes police brutality. I have heard them called the new Jews. That analogy is not useful, since Muslims in today's western Europe have never been massacred by Christian crusaders, expelled from one country after another, forced to wear distinctive dress, barred from many professions, or systematically slaughtered by Nazis. In fact, right now, some Muslim militants are among the chief purveyors of anti-Semitism in Europe (they get a lot of help from neo-fascists). In America, the "new Jews" label clearly doesn't work. According to FBI statistics, between 2002 and 2011 there were 1,388 hate crimes committed against American Muslims and 9,198 against American Jews—and 25,130 against black Americans.[3] The age of Trump has brought significant increases in hate crimes generally, most of all in crimes against Muslims, but the overall statistics have not changed much.[4] The left should defend all hate crime victims, but it isn't wrong to recognize where the greatest dangers lie.

After the Paris attacks of 2015, the Brussels attacks of 2016, and the migrant crisis produced by the Syrian and Iraqi civil wars, it is clear that Europe's Muslims (and to a lesser extent America's) are a minority in trouble. The trouble is caused in part by the jihadi terrorists in their midst, but it is also caused by police actions against innocent Muslims and by the popular response to the terrorists. Muslims today rightly receive sympathy and support from the European left, which also hopes, rightly again, to win their votes as they become citizens. Many right-wing groups campaign against all Muslims—not only far-right splinter groups like the English Defense League or Germany's Die Freiheit and Pro-Deutschland, but populist parties that command considerable electoral support, like the National Front in France and the Party for Freedom in the Netherlands. Since the political leaders of all these groups claim to fear the rise of Islam in Europe, Islamophobia has become politically incorrect for everyone on the left. What is much more important, it is morally wrong.

At issue is not only fear but also hatred: Islamophobia is a version of religious intolerance, and leftists must oppose the bigots in Europe and the United States who deliberately misunderstand and misrepresent contemporary Islam. Islamophobes on the right insist that jihadi zealotry is an inevitable product of Islamic theology; they make no distinction between historical Islam and the zealots of this moment; they regard every Muslim immigrant in a Western country as a potential terrorist; and they fail to acknowledge, if they even know, the towering achievements of Muslim philosophers, poets, and artists over many centuries. Consider, for example, the Dutch nationalist Geert Wilders, leader of the Party for Freedom, who describes the Qur'an as a "fascist book" and calls for it to be outlawed (like *Mein Kampf*) in The Netherlands. Or Hans-Jürgen Irmer, deputy floor leader of the Christian Democratic Union in Hesse, Germany, who claims that "Islam is set on global domination."[5] There are indeed Islamists with global ambitions (even in Germany—remember Mohamed Atta), but we don't hold all Muslims responsible for Islamist zealotry any more than we hold all Hindus responsible for Hindutva zealotry or all Christians responsible for Christian zealotry. People like Wilders and Irmer (and our own Donald Trump) go a long way in explaining the left's strong aversion to Islamophobia.

But we have to be careful. Perfectly legitimate criticisms can be made not only of Islamist zealots but also of Islam itself—as of every religion. Pascal Bruckner argues that the term "Islamophobia" was "a clever invention because it amounts to making Islam a subject that one cannot touch without being accused of racism."[6] The term was first used, he claims, to condemn Kate Millet for calling upon Iranian women to take off their chadors. I hope there are critics of Islam who escape the accusation, but it is certainly true that even internal critics, Muslim liberals and secularists like the novelist Kamal Daoud, have been called Islamophobic by left intellectuals in the West.[7] So it is worth repeating Bruckner's point: there has to be room for feminists like Millet and for atheists, philosophical skeptics, Enlightenment liberals, and all others to say their piece about Islam, and about Christianity and Judaism, and to find an audience if they can. We can call them to account for bad arguments, but their critical work is normal and should be welcomed in a free society.

The critique of Islam and Islamism is inhibited not only by fear of Islamophobia but also by fear of "Orientalism." Edward Said's book by that name provides many examples of both scholarly and popular arguments about Islam that contemporary writers will rightly want to avoid. But his own argument about the future of Islam and the Arab world (he was writing in the late 1970s) missed the mark by a good distance. Said thought that with only a few honorable exceptions, Orientalism had triumphed—and not only in the West. It had also been internalized in the East, so Arab and other Muslim writers were now producing Orientalist accounts of their own history. In his words: "The Arab world today is an intellectual, political, and cultural satellite of the United States." Islamic revivalism is nowhere anticipated in Said's book. Indeed, he takes Bernard Lewis's insistence on the "importance of religion in the current affairs of the Muslim world" to be a prime example of Orientalism.[8] A year later, in *The Question of Palestine*, Said calls "the return to Islam" a "chimera."[9] It would be difficult for anyone to say that now (Said stopped saying it in later years), but it is still rare for writers on the left to address the chimera head on.

The critique of Islam and of Islamism is constrained these days. Islamophobia, however, seems to be growing, and the popularity of the populist or nationalist right is worrying. Why is this happening? The new *Islamophobia Studies Journal*, a biannual publication sponsored by Berkeley's Center for Race and Gender, identifies the source of the trouble in an editorial:

> For some, rising anti-Muslim sentiments are immediately explained away as a "natural" outcome of the many violent events in the Muslim world and "terrorism" in general. However, we maintain that the rising negative sentiments may have to do with the presence of a well-organized and well-funded Islamophobic industry that has managed to invade and capture civil society and public discourses without serious contestation. Up to this point, anti-racist and progressive voices have not been effective in challenging this industry, nor have they been able to provide the needed resources to mount regional and national responses.[10]

This is nicely self-serving: more resources for the *Journal* would be a big help in combating the Islamophobia industry. But how about the reluctance to engage with "the many violent events in the Muslim world"?

A similar reluctance occurs in a series of otherwise excellent articles published in a special issue of *The Nation* in July 2012. Jack Shaheen's "How the Media Created the Muslim Monster Myth" offers an argument very much like that of the editors of the *Islamophobia Studies Journal*. The novelist Laila Lalami, in "Islamophobia and Its Discontents," recognizes that "retrograde blasphemy laws" and "unfair divorce laws" may have something to do with hostility to Islam, but she rightly refuses to treat these as excuses for the harassment she has lived with here in the United States. Nor does Islamist violence, which she doesn't discuss, provide any such excuse. I want to be clear about this: European and American prejudice against Muslims should never be justified by pointing to Islamist zealotry. But the entirely legitimate desire to avoid prejudice isn't a reason to run away from talking about the zealots.

What can explain the refusal of "anti-racist and progressive voices" to sound an alarm about "violent events in the Muslim world"? Isn't it strange that most of the denunciations of Islamophobia refer only to fearful, hostile, or critical Europeans and Americans and virtually ignore what is happening in countries where Muslims are a huge majority—and where infidels and heretics often find themselves in desperate trouble? In fact, I did find a discussion of these issues in the *Daily Sabah*, a pro-Erdogan Turkish website, which recently carried an article by Hatem Bazian (a member of the Berkeley faculty and one of the founders of the *Islamophobia Studies Journal*) called "Deconstructing Islamophobia in Muslim Majority States."[11] Bazian argues that in many Muslim-majority states, Islamophobia is a colonialist, "orientalist" hangover, exploited and augmented by secularist elites educated "in Western epistemologies." He is pointing, I suppose, at secularists like those young Egyptians who began the revolt against Mubarak and mobilized against the Muslim Brotherhood—but who aren't enough of an elite to govern the country. Those Egyptians are not Islamophobic; they fear the Islamists, not Islam, and surely they have reason to be afraid.

A Strange Left

Most leftists, whatever problems they have understanding religion, have no difficulty opposing Hindu nationalists, zealous Buddhist monks, and the messianic Zionists of the settler movement. Nor does anyone on the left make common cause with Islamist militants who kidnap schoolgirls, murder heretics, or tear down ancient monuments. Acts like these, insofar as they are noticed, are routinely condemned. Well, not quite routinely: Nikolas Kozloff, in a *Huffington Post* article entitled "A Tale of Boko Haram, Political Correctness, Feminism, and the Left," has documented some leftists' strange unwillingness to blame Muslim zealots for the kidnapping of the Nigerian schoolgirls.[12] Less outrageous, but bad enough, is the unwillingness of many more leftists, who recognize this and other crimes, to attempt an encompassing critique of Islamist zealotry. What stands in the way?

Deepa Kumar's book on Islamophobia suggests a possible answer. What stands in the way is that Islamists are opponents of "the West," that is, of Western, really American, "imperialism": bases in Saudi Arabia, the war in Afghanistan, the two Iraq wars, the Libyan intervention, support for Israel, drone strikes in Somalia, and so on. This list, it seems to me, requires a selective response—opposition in some cases, certainly, but agreement in others. I dare say that the overthrow by Islamist zealots of US-supported regimes in the Middle East, bad as some of them are, would not be terribly helpful to the people of the region. But most leftist opponents of imperialism don't make selective judgments. What I call the politics of distinction has little appeal—though more and more leftists are ready to distinguish ISIS from earlier Islamist groups; its brutality is too emphatic and too visible to be excused. But the "enemy of my enemy" maxim still holds in other cases. We saw it invoked in the August 2015 demonstrations in London in support of Hamas, which brought together secular leftists—fierce opponents of Islamophobia—and religious Muslims.

Another reason for the reluctance to condemn Islamist crimes is the great eagerness to condemn the crimes of the West. The root cause of religious zealotry is not religion, many leftist writers insist, but Western imperialism and the oppression and poverty it has bred. So, for example, David Swanson, on the War Is a Crime website and then on the Tikkun website (with a nervous but only partial disclaimer from the editor), asks, "What to do about ISIS?" and answers: "Start by recognizing where ISIS came from. The US and its junior partners destroyed Iraq."[13] In other words, there would be no ISIS without the US invasion of Iraq in 2003. That may (or may not) be a true account of ISIS's success in Iraq, but it isn't generally true. ISIS didn't come from the US invasion; it is a product of the worldwide religious revival. Swanson might offer a similar explanation for all the other examples of revivalist militancy, but the explanation grows less convincing as the instances multiply.

Similarly, Lindsey German, of the UK Stop the War Coalition (chaired in recent years by Jeremy Corbyn), argues in the *Guardian* (May 6, 2014) that the rise of Boko Haram is the unintended work of the West: "If Islamism is now a threat to Western interests in . . . parts of Africa, it is one they have played a large part in creating." Boko Haram, in this view, isn't a threat primarily to Nigerian schoolgirls but to Western business interests; it is a response to oppression, corruption, and economic injustice. Addressing similar views on the excellent website Left Foot Forward, Leo Igwe insists that "any intelligent member of Nigerian society" knows that Boko Haram doesn't speak for poor or marginalized Nigerians. Its "campaign of violence and bloodletting is rooted in its fanatical interpretation and appropriation of Islam."[14]

But the left's more common view of root causes doesn't include religion. Aren't all religions the ideological tools of the ruling class? Aren't all millennialist and messianic uprisings the ideologically distorted response of subaltern groups to material oppression? Religious zealotry is a superstructural phenomenon that can be explained only by reference to the economic base. These ancient convictions are particularly unhelpful today. Parvez Ahmed, who writes frequently and insightfully for the *Huffington Post* and who is fully cognizant of the "scourge" of Boko Haram, provides a typical example: "Much of the violence [committed] in the name of Islam," he argues, "is less motivated by faith and more by poverty and desperation."[15] If this is right, why don't poverty and desperation produce a leftist rather than an Islamist mobilization? In fact, the religious revival, not only among Muslims but around the world among Jews and Christians, Hindus and Buddhists, has enlisted supporters from all social classes, and its driving motive seems, incredibly, to be religious faith. (Fawaz Gerges's book *Journey of the Jihadist* provides ample evidence of religion's power.)[16]

Many people on the left believe that Islamist zealotry not only is produced by Western imperialism but is a form of resistance to it. Whatever groups it attracts, they argue, it is fundamentally an ideology of the oppressed—a version, though a little strange, of left politics. The brutality of ISIS militants has made this view increasingly hard to defend. But many leftist writers have described the Sunni and Shi'ite militias fighting against the US occupation of Iraq as "the resistance." Susan Watkins, editor of *New Left Review*, called them "the Iraqi maquis," deliberately invoking the French Resistance to the Nazis in World War II.[17] Nothing about the Islamist militias was leftist, however, except that they were fighting against Americans. Fred Halliday, in an article in *Dissent* called "The Jihadism of Fools," objected to the word "resistance" and other similar usages.[18] The title of his article is a good tag, but it didn't stick, as we can see from Slavoj Žižek's claim the following year that Islamic radicalism is "the rage of the victims of capitalist globalization." I have to acknowledge that Žižek is not afraid to be called Islamophobic; he advocates a "respectful, but for that reason no less ruthless" critique of Islam.[19] But he won't get the critique right as long as he thinks that the object of Islamist rage is the same as the object of his own rage.

Judith Butler made a similar mistake in 2006 when she insisted that "understanding Hamas [and] Hezbollah as social movements that are progressive, that are on the left, that are part of the global left, is extremely important." She repeated this assertion with interesting amendments in 2012: Hamas and Hezbollah belong to the global left because they are "anti-imperialist," but she doesn't support every organization on the global left, and she specifically doesn't endorse the use of violence by those two.[20] That last amendment is welcome, but the left identification was as wrong in 2012 as it was in 2006—usefully wrong, perhaps, since it helps explain why so many leftists support or won't actively oppose groups like Hamas and Hezbollah. What makes these organizations "leftist" is that they are fighting against Israel, which stands in, as it often does, for imperial America.

What would a genuinely leftist movement against oppression and poverty look like—in the Islamic world or anywhere else? What kind of movement should evoke expressions of solidarity and material support from American leftists, human rights advocates, feminists, and labor unionists? First of all, it would have to be a movement *of the oppressed*, not of some vanguard claiming to speak for the oppressed. It would be a mobilization of men and women, previously passive and inarticulate, now able to speak for themselves and defend their rights. Second, its aim would be the liberation or, better, the self-emancipation of those people. Its driving force would be a vision, no doubt partially shaped by the local culture, of a new society whose members, men and women alike, would be more free and more equal and whose government would be responsive and accountable. Surely that's not an unusual description of left aspiration. How, then, can anyone seriously believe that any of the Islamist groups belong to the global, or any other, left?

The post-modernists haven't done any better than the anti-imperialists in explaining their support for Islamist zealotry. Michel Foucault's romance with the Iranian revolution is an old story by now, but his response to the revolution's brutality—Iran doesn't "have the same regime of truth as ours"[21]—is an early example of a position now too common on the left. Foucault's response is memorably different from that of the Egyptian left/liberal philosopher Zaki Najib Mahmud, who also wrote in the late 1970s: "I rub my eyes and think I am living through a nightmare . . . I had to live to see the fundamentalists clamor for cutting off the hands of thieves, for stoning the adulterous, and similar penalties, which run counter to the spirit of our age!"[22] Mahmud's is a left response that sounds right to me, despite the claim, which I can no longer make, that the age is ours. Now consider the case of Azar Nafisi, the author of *Reading Lolita in Tehran*, a lovely account of cultural subversion in an Islamist state. In exile in the United States, she told an interviewer in Boston, "I very much resent it in the West when people—maybe with good intentions or from a progressive point of view—keep telling me, 'It's their culture.' . . . It's like saying, the culture of Massachusetts is burning witches. There are aspects of culture that are really reprehensible. . . . We shouldn't accept them."[23] Those well-intentioned and progressive people are probably advocates of a radical multiculturalism—which might well allow the burning of witches so long as it doesn't happen in Massachusetts. The post-modern political theorist Anne Norton, in *On the Muslim Question*, defends deep cultural differences, a stance that is politically correct (and also right), but she manages to avoid serious engagement with anything really reprehensible (which isn't right). In any case, she is sure that the West is worse.[24] What we see here, writes Dan Diner in *Lost in the Sacred*, is "an unholy alliance between *premodern* conditions still prevalent in the Middle East and an apologetic *postmodern* discourse that has established itself in the West."[25] This alliance precludes any close encounter with actual events.

The strongest post-modern defense of Islamic radicalism comes from Michael Hardt and Antonio Negri, who argue that Islamism is itself a post-modern project: "The postmodernity of fundamentalism has to be recognized primarily in its refusal of modernity as a weapon of Euro-American hegemony—and in this regard Islamic fundamentalism is indeed the paradigmatic case." And again: "Insofar as the Iranian revolution was a powerful rejection of the world market, we might think of it as the first postmodern revolution."[26] Is it cruel of me to point out how eager the Iranians are these days to rejoin the world market?

All these left responses to Islamist zealots—identification, support, sympathy, apology, tolerance, and avoidance—look very strange if we consider the content of Islamist ideology (theology, in fact, but most leftists are theologically tone-deaf). Jihadi opposition to the West should provoke serious worry on the left before any other response. Boko Haram began with an attack on Western-style schools, and other Islamist groups have undertaken similar attacks, especially on schools for girls. Among the values the zealots denounce as Western are individual liberty, democracy, gender equality, and religious pluralism. Westerners don't always live in accordance with these values and often fail to defend them when they need defense, but Western hypocrisy pays tribute to them—and some of us Westerners struggle to uphold them.

In the years since the fall of Soviet communism, Russia and China have sometimes claimed to oppose both Western imperialism and Western values, but these two countries look more like rival imperial powers than opponents of imperialism. While their leaders occasionally resort to value arguments (as when Chinese rulers endorse the Confucian ideal of harmony), they don't seem strongly committed to the values they proclaim. But most Islamists are committed. They have their own large ambitions, but highly idealistic ones. No doubt, their idealism leaves room for political maneuver, but it leaves very little room for material interests. Their zealotry is a value zealotry, theologically driven, and it is a real challenge to Western values.

But individual liberty, democracy, gender equality, and religious pluralism aren't really Western values; they are universal values that first appeared in strong, modern versions in western Europe and the Americas. They pretty much define the left, which also first appeared in its strong, modern version in western Europe and the Americas. The left is an eighteenth-century invention, a product of the secular Enlightenment. There were people who held potentially leftist positions in all the major religious traditions—pacifists, communitarians, proto-environmentalists, vegetarians, advocates for the poor, even people who believed in equality or, more often, in the equal standing of all believers before God (I should probably say, all male believers). But nothing like the classic left ever existed among religious Hindus, Jews, Buddhists, Muslims, or Christians. The values of the left are those "Western" values, the ones I just listed, taken very seriously. Opposition to those values is something the left should take on, as we readily do when the opposition comes from the far right. But this very same opposition is the reason many leftists are reluctant to take on the Islamist radicals.

A Better Left

How should the left respond to Islamism today? I am not going to consider military responses here. There is, as I suggested at the beginning of this chapter, something like an International Brigade of

Islamist zealots, recruited from many countries, fighting right now in Iraq and Syria, but there is no chance of recruiting an International Brigade of leftist fighters, so there is no point thinking about where we might send them. Leftists must support (though many won't) military efforts specifically aimed at stopping the massacre of infidels and heretics. After that, I am more inclined to consider a policy focused on the containment of Islamism rather than a war, or a series of wars, to destroy it. The Islamist fever will have to burn itself out. The problem is that many people will suffer in the burning, and leftists will ignore their suffering at our moral peril. How to help those people is a question we will have to address again and again. But we should begin with the ideological war.

In that war, we need to practice the politics of distinction; we need to distinguish carefully between Islamist zealotry and Islam itself, or Islam at its best. The doctrines of ISIS derive from a possible interpretation of the Qur'an and the traditions that follow from it—just as the doctrines of the messianic Zionists of the Israeli settler movement can plausibly be described as interpretations of the Jewish tradition. But we have to insist that these interpretations are perverse; there are better ones that hew more closely to the two traditions' central values. I doubt we will get any credit for insisting. Writers like Paul Berman and Meredith Tax have made this argument scrupulously in everything they have written against the Islamists, and their critics have mostly managed not to notice. No one else's care is likely to be noticed, but the argument is important. We should insist particularly on the difference between the writings of zealots like Hassan al-Banna and Sayyid Qutb in Egypt and Maulana Mawdudi in India, on the one hand, and, on the other, the work of the great rationalist philosophers of the Muslim past or the liberal reformers of more recent times. We should do this in exactly the same way as we would distinguish between the preachings of the Christian Crusades and Scholastic theology.

We should also engage cooperatively with Muslim and lapsed Muslim opponents of zealotry and give them the support they ask for. There are a lot of these anti-zealots, some of whom, like Ayaan Hirsi Ali, started on the left and then moved rightward in part because they found so few leftist friends. Paul Berman has written a withering critique of the treatment of Hirsi Ali by leading liberal/left intellectuals, and Katha Pollitt, writing in *The Nation*, wondered courageously whether "we leftists and feminists need to think a bit more self-critically about how the American Enterprise Institute [a neo-conservative think tank] . . . managed to win over this bold and complex crusader for women's rights."[27] We would definitely benefit from a study of Hirsi Ali's trajectory, which was driven in large part by the left's fear of Islamophobia. There is a strange unwillingness among leftists to welcome atheists emerging from the Muslim world in the way we would welcome atheists emerging from, say, the Christian world.

Besides distinguishing Islam from Islamist zealotry in our politics, we have to acknowledge that the academic theory (also a left theory) that predicted the inevitable triumph of science and secularism isn't right—at least its time horizon isn't right. Leftists have to figure out how to defend the secular state in this apparently post-secular age and how to defend equality and democracy against religious arguments for hierarchy and theocracy. The appeal of religious doctrine and practice is obvious, and we need to understand it if we are to persuade people that religious zealotry is frighteningly unappealing.

We also need to move beyond theory by recognizing the zealots' power and the extent of their political reach. We should clearly name the zealots our enemies and commit ourselves to an intellectual campaign against them—that is, a campaign in defense of liberty, democracy, equality, and pluralism. I am not arguing that leftists should join Samuel Huntington's famous "clash of civilizations." Nick Cohen's line is worth remembering: "All faiths in their extreme form carry the possibility of tyranny." All the great religious civilizations are capable, probably equally capable, of producing violent fanatics and peace-loving saints—and everything in between. So we shouldn't think about the struggle with Islamists in civilizational but rather in ideological terms. The ideology we should be defending is secularist but not anti-religious; we are not at war with the faithful—not with all of them. Many devout Muslims support the universal values of the West and the left—and find those values in Islamic texts just as other religious leftists find them in Hindu, Jewish, and Christian texts.

The organization Women Living under Muslim Laws (WLUML), which works in many Muslim majority countries, is effectively engaged in just this search, with special regard to gender equality. That issue is especially important: fear of liberated women is one of the key causes of the religious revival, and subordination of women is one of the key goals of religious zealotry. So liberated women are important members of the global left. The women of WLUML have shown remarkable strength in what are often hostile environments and deserve more support than they have gotten from today's leftists. The WLUML statement at the 2005 World Social Forum in Porto Alegre, Brazil, exemplifies what should be a common position:

> Fundamentalist terror is by no means a tool of the poor against the rich, of the Third World against the West, of people against capitalism. It is not a legitimate response that can be supported by the progressive forces of the world. Its main target is the internal democratic opposition to [its] theocratic project . . . of controlling all aspects of society in the name of religion. . . . When fundamentalists come to power, they silence the people; they physically eliminate dissidents . . . they lock women "in

their place," which as we know from experience ends up being a strait jacket.[28]

This reads like an appeal against Halliday's jihadism of fools, and I am sure there were foolish people at the World Social Forum who accused WLUML of Islamophobia.

Secular feminists have also mobilized against religiously motivated misogyny—including the Islamists' irrational fear of women: see, for example, the website of the Center for Secular Space. I think of WLUML and the center as examples of an internationalist feminism. Strangely, the left in general is much more ready to embrace a feminism that focuses on domestic politics—as if gender equality were not only a Western idea but an idea applicable only in the West.

The secular left responds to some forms of religious extremism with appropriate hostility—it responds especially well to extremism at home. But its response to Islamism abroad has been hesitant and often misguided. Again, why is this so? The fear of Islamophobia is one important reason, and I have suggested a set of additional, related reasons: because Islamists oppose the West, because the West is supposedly responsible for Islamist violence (among many more bad things), and because we Westerners have no right to criticize the way "they" do things over there. There are probably other reasons. How to respond to religious radicalism should be a question of critical interest to leftists wherever they live, but it hasn't received anything like the attention it deserves. With regard to religion, as in many other regards, we need a more engaged, intelligent, and militant internationalism.

As I've already noted, there is no chance that an International Brigade of leftist fighters will join any of today's military battles. My friends and neighbors are not ready to enlist; many of them won't acknowledge the extent of the dangers posed by religious zealotry. But there are dangers, and the secular left needs defenders. For those of us who are writers, not fighters, the most helpful thing we can do is to join the ideological wars. We can claim comrades in many nations, but not yet anywhere near enough of them. The International Brigade of left intellectuals is still waiting to take shape.

EIGHT

The Complex Formation of Our Battles

I have ended every chapter in this book with programmatic arguments, which I sum up here in a few pointed sentences.

- Leftists here at home need to seek out, listen to, and work with comrades abroad—and comrades are only those men and women who are as committed as we are to freedom and equality. We must never become the comrades of tyrants, oligarchs, or terrorists.
- We have to learn to support the use of force *sometimes*—when it is needed to stop a massacre, say, or resist aggression, even if the army engaged in those efforts is the army of a capitalist state. We must work for peace whenever peace is possible, but we must practice the politics of distinction by opposing wars of conquest and supporting wars of self-defense and the defense of others.
- We have to be honest in describing authoritarian regimes, including those that call themselves leftist—and we have

to be tough-minded and realistic in discussing the effectiveness of global governance. We must reject the politics of pretending.

- Without becoming anti-American Americans, we have to work for the limitation of American hegemony, for compromise (a Gramscian equilibrium), and a global division of labor. We have to tell our allies abroad that they, too, are responsible for the way the world goes.
- Together with those allies, we should be committed to an internationalism of agency. The relief of global poverty and the repair of global injustice should aim at producing men and women capable of helping themselves and determining their own political future. That requires us to support what I've called the completion of the state system, so that everyone who needs a decent state has one—a state that belongs to all its citizens and provides them with security and welfare. The state is right now, though not forever, the necessary agent of a common life.
- But we also need to aim at a politics beyond the sovereign state—stronger global institutions underpinned by an international civil society in which people like us can work for all the causes of the left. That work has no end; it is our permanent politics.
- Finally, we must resist the political regression that religious zealots seek to impose, and defend the "Western" values that they attack—which we insist are universal values.

All that, taken together, constitutes the foreign policy of the left. None of the arguments I have made are original; I think of them as pedestrian arguments, leftist commonplaces. But at every point, making them has required me to criticize other versions of leftism.

Some of these criticisms represent what I hope are useful disagreements. But some invoke a frustrating sense of failure and defeat. The hopes with which the left began the twentieth century, the hopes renewed after the cataclysm of World War II, after the Holocaust, after the defeat of Nazism, after we learned to worry, have come to—what? There are some real achievements, always politically incomplete and geographically limited: social-democracy, national liberation, feminism. But the left is much weaker than we thought it would be, and the world is much as it was. What we always considered the forces of reaction—the hierarchs, oligarchs, and patriarchs; the economic and political predators; the corporate magnates; the tyrants, warlords, and militarists—are still powerful, still hard at work, dominant in too many places. And the passive and inarticulate men and women who were supposed to become politically engaged, self-determining citizens, committed to equality and democracy, are still mostly passive and inarticulate—or they turn out to have commitments that we didn't anticipate and can't support.

So the left encounters resistance; we should have expected that. But I don't want to write about the resistance, not here; I want to write about the left. Why haven't we done better in this world-historical encounter?

Albert Camus provides what I think is the strongest answer: "The great event of the twentieth century," he argues, "was the forsaking of the values of freedom by the revolutionary movements."[1] Leftists created tyrannical regimes, monstrous regimes, which other leftists defended. Yes, still others among us criticized those regimes, but for many years the dominant form of left politics required the support of tyrants: Stalin, Mao, and a long string of third world dictators. There was an argument behind this support that we need to engage. Only dictatorship, we were told again and again, could overcome the forces of reaction and their long-entrenched hierarchical structures; only dictatorship could promote equality. Social-democrats and bourgeois liberals would compromise endlessly and never reach the radical transformation they pretended to support; they lacked the rough energy, the necessary brutality. It would take a Maximal Leader, a determined vanguard, to do the required work.

But this argument has one major difficulty: dictatorship is, first and foremost, a violation of equality; it isn't a means for eradicating hierarchy but an enactment of it. This is so because dictatorship is constituted by an unequal distribution of political power: the one or the few have it and the many don't. And inequality in the political sphere has never failed to lead to inequality everywhere else. The dictator himself (or, rarely, herself), his relatives, and his cronies or the vanguard militants and their political friends—all these people will amass for themselves and their children the rewards of political power. If the old oligarchs are overthrown, new oligarchs are soon in place. William Butler Yeats provides a warning about revolutions that change the personnel but not the structure of hierarchical relations:

> Hurrah for revolution and more cannon-shot!
> A beggar upon horseback lashes a beggar on foot.
> Hurrah for revolution and cannon come again!
> The beggars have changed places, but the lash goes on.[2]

That freedom and equality are necessarily in conflict was originally a right-wing argument. The left took it over at its peril. Right-wingers mean to defend economic liberty: laissez-faire capitalism and the society it produces. This kind of liberty is indeed in conflict with equality. Political liberty is not. The left must always defend democratic government and the freedoms of press and association that it requires, which make the fight for an egalitarian society possible. It may be true that a leftist dictatorship can confiscate property and defeat the corporate elite, while the democratic struggle against inequality is harder and slower. But that struggle is our politics. The shortcuts promised by ideological vanguards and populist leaders always end up creating a new privileged class— which requires a renewed oppositional struggle, harder and more dangerous than democratic politics, in which we are turned from movement activists into dissidents, hiding from the secret police.

We can think of democracy as the means for the creation of a socialist society, but that is only part of the story. We need political freedom to fight for the containment of capitalism, the strengthening of the public sphere, and the provision of welfare, but we need all these for the fulfillment of democracy. "Democracy," Hayim Greenberg wrote in 1941, "is the ultimate goal and socialism is, under modern industrial conditions, the practical means for the attainment of this goal." The society we hope to create won't represent a transcendence of politics, as Marxists once predicted; there will still be "tensions, conflicts, and contradictions which will have to be solved by citizens enjoying equal rights and equal social standing according to some established democratic procedure."[3] And in the process of solving the contradictions, we (leftists) will sometimes win political victories, sometimes lose, and sometimes be forced into compromises that fall short of our goals. We must beware of revolutionaries who promise solutions that never fall short: they are almost certainly asking us to forsake the values of freedom.

Two-Front Wars

In World War II, in 1943 and early '44, we all waited hopefully for the opening of a second front—an Allied attack on Nazi Germany through France to match the Soviet army's advance from the east. The fighting in North Africa and Italy didn't do the job; it was the landing in Normandy that established the two-front war. But this was a war on two fronts against one enemy. We were the allies of Stalinist Russia, and this alliance was politically and morally necessary (although it probably wasn't necessary to call Stalin "Uncle Joe" and pretend he was a good democrat). There were people, not a lot of them, who supported the war against the Nazis, who fought in the war, but who sustained a strong opposition to British and French imperialism and to Soviet totalitarianism. They were politically engaged on three fronts. Most often, two is enough, but not always.

The kind of political war I want to defend goes back to the French Revolution. There, members of the Girondin faction, men like Brissot and Condorcet, fought against the king and his supporters at home and abroad and against the Jacobin zealots to their left. The designations "left" and "right" come from those days; the Jacobins were the first leftists—and also the first revolutionary movement to forsake the values of freedom. Girondin politicians and philosophes were the better defenders of those values and, over the long run, of equality and democracy too.

The Mensheviks fought a similar two-front war for similar reasons. When they were defeated by the Bolsheviks and driven into exile, the global left, including the American left, mostly lost interest in them or treated them with contempt—as if losing was a sign of revolutionary feebleness or faithlessness. The catchphrase "no enemies to the left" dates from the French Revolution (*pas d'ennemis à gauche*), but it was most effective and most damaging to left politics during and after the Russian revolution. It mandates a refusal to fight on more than one front, a refusal to recognize more than one enemy. The history of the twentieth century is one long terrifying argument against this refusal.

The greatest crime of the twentieth century was the Nazi effort to exterminate the Jews—greatest because it was a genocide, the systematic murder of men, women, and children simply because they shared a religious and national identity, and worse, a genocide that came frighteningly close to complete success. But make no mistake: it was the left that killed the greater number of people between 1918 and the 1970s—from the Bolshevik seizure of power in Russia to Stalin's purges to the murderous reign of Mao Zedong in China to the Khmer Rouge killing fields in Cambodia. Revolutionary murder wasn't as focused or systematic—or as nearly successful—as Nazi genocide, but it proceeded on a monstrous scale for many more years.[4] And too many leftists around the world defended it—or else practiced an extreme example of the politics of pretending: denying the killings and insisting that the reports were all capitalist propaganda. In much the same way, many Germans after 1945 pretended that they hadn't known about the death camps. They knew, and so did Stalin's and Mao's apologists. If this last sad assembly of leftists thought the fight against capitalist exploitation was all that mattered, they were terribly wrong.

I am a very old leftist, and when I insist on this account of twentieth-century history, I often encounter resistance, skepticism, or impatience among young people on today's left. That's old news, they say. What does it have to do with us? It has everything to do with us, because the us that matters encompasses more than one generation. The left is its history as well as its daily presence and current concerns. Its weakness today derives from its failures yesterday. If we don't engage with those failures, we will repeat them.

Some of us are already repeating them. The continuing support for terrorists who call themselves leftists—and even for some, like the Iraqi maquis, who don't—is one such failure. But what is more troubling is the growing acceptance in the left academy of leftist tyranny. The subjects of revisionist approval are entirely familiar: the French Terror, Stalinist repression, Mao's cultural revolution.[5] Only the language of these academics is new: willfully obscure, seemingly paradoxical, jokey, and cleverly designed to allow deniability. Slavoj

Žižek is the most prolific and best known of these leftists, and perhaps the most evasive. Sometimes his intent is clear: "There are no 'democratic (procedural) rules' one is a priori prohibited to violate," he writes; "revolutionary politics is not a matter of opinions but of the truth on behalf of which one often is compelled to disregard the 'opinion of the majority' and to impose the revolutionary will against it." He wants to "resignify" terror—"the ruthless exercise of power, the spirit of sacrifice."[6] I am not sure whether Žižek himself is titillated by violence or simply aims to titillate his readers. He has succeeded in this second project, as Adam Kirsch has pointed out: "The louder he applauds violence and terror—especially the terror of Lenin, Stalin, and Mao . . . the more indulgently he is received by the academic left, which has elevated him into a celebrity and the center of a cult."[7]

The cultic behavior of the left academy probably isn't very important, and Žižek's writings have been sharply criticized by leftists like Alan Johnson and Paul Bowman in Britain, who are still committed to the values of the left.[8] But Žižek and his followers remind us of battles lost in the last century that must not be lost again. When Voltaire signed his letters with "ecrasez l'infame" (let us crush the infamous), his targets were the Church, the Inquisition, the religious zealots of his time. We still have enemies of that sort, and I haven't forgotten the domestic left's primary targets—inequality and plutocracy—which must figure also in our choice of comrades and causes abroad. But we won't be successful anywhere if we don't come to grips with revolutionary terror and dictatorship: our own infamy.

The Complex Formation of Our Battles

How should we fight on our several fronts? I wrote earlier about the Vietnam years, when it was necessary to oppose the American war and yet refuse to support the other side. Here is an example of the complex formation of our battles. By the time of the initial American engagement, the Vietcong had already assassinated most of the independent leftists in the South, but there were still people in Saigon whom we should have been in touch with, asking, "How can we help?" We should have called for the creation in Saigon of a decent government that might be capable of rallying the people of the South against the looming communist victory. But we had to recognize that the actual governments the United States created or propped up could not do that, and that our opposition to the war had a necessary and very ugly consequence. The communists had won the battle for hearts and minds and would, when the Americans finally withdrew, establish a tyrannical regime. Nonetheless, we had to argue for American withdrawal, for the war had become a greater crime than the coming tyranny. But we also had to insist that the withdrawal include not only our soldiers but also our collaborators, all the men and women whom our war had put at risk. And then, after a withdrawal that left most of them behind, we had to defend the boat people, who were trying to escape, and criticize North Vietnamese murder and "reeducation." These are only some of the complicated political and moral requirements of those years. It was easy to get lost.

Now consider the invasion of Iraq in 2003 and the ongoing war in the years since. As I wrote in chapter 1, there were people on the left, here in the United States, in Europe, and among the Iraqi exiles, who supported the invasion, but the larger left opposed it. I was one of those in opposition, chiefly because regime change (the main goal of pro-war leftists) has never struck me as a just cause for sending an army across an international frontier—except when a rebellion is already in progress and there is a government-in-waiting. A sustained rebellion and a government ready to rule demonstrate that regime change is well begun and is being promoted by local forces with a popular base. Even then, it would be better if the insurgents won on their own or with the help of an International Brigade, but I can see a leftist argument for sending in an army (this argument might, retrospectively, justify the French intervention in the American Revolution). In Iraq in 2003, however, there was no locally initiated rebellion and no popularly based government-in-waiting; the American invasion was a war that it was right to oppose.

For most leftists, however, opposing the war and then the American occupation was pretty much the sum of their politics. Many things went terribly wrong in Iraq after the three-week American military victory, and the standard left response was to blame the Americans for all the calamities and to cheer for any Iraqis who resisted the occupation. What the US Army accomplished in those three weeks was the overthrow of a brutal tyrant. After that, the American effort to rule the country was, as Kenan Makiya has written, "brainless" and, I would add, unjust.[9] An ongoing critique from the left was certainly necessary. But the sectarian wars that devastated the country were the responsibility of the sects and their leaders, not of the Americans. The wars were connected to a global revival of Islamist militancy that began well before 2003.

Something else happened after the invasion, unexpected by the left but requiring leftist attention: space was opened not only for the sects but also for Iraqi trade unionists, secular democrats, and feminists. These people needed and deserved our help. They certainly weren't helped by the American administrators of the occupation, who were mostly intent on the creation of a friendly regime and a "free-enterprise" economy. Nor did they get help from the international left. In Britain, a group called Labour Friends of Iraq provided strong support for Iraqi unionists—who were, however, consistently condemned on the farther left, most sharply by the Stop the War Coalition, because they were not part of the resistance. Labour Friends of Iraq provided a nice example of the required two-front war: it opposed the resistance while sharply criticizing the occupation and the conduct of the US Army.

In the United States, the Solidarity Center of the AFL-CIO supported efforts of Iraqi unions to rewrite Saddam Hussein's labor laws, while American companies doing business in Iraq brought with them the anti-union practices they had developed at home. This conflict between capitalist and union politics, in which one side was obviously leftist, found little resonance on the wider American left.

The story of Iraqi feminism is sadly similar: a surge of energy and organization immediately after the invasion found virtually no response, no effective support, from the Western left. Here I will follow (and conclude with) the argument of Nadje Al-Ali's "A Feminist Perspective on the Iraq War" published in 2011.[10] Al-Ali stands somewhere to my left as a "transnational feminist antimilitarist," but she is "suspicious of [the] dichotomous narratives and mono-causal explanations" promoted by many of her fellow leftists, and for that reason her writing seems to me profoundly instructive.

Al-Ali fought steadily against the sanctions imposed on Iraq after the Kuwait war of 1990, against the American invasion of 2003, and against the occupation that followed. She sustained at the same time a fierce anger against people on the left who "glorified the Ba'ath regime and [the] dictatorship of Saddam Hussein" and, later on, called the "killing of Iraqi civilians, foreign humanitarian workers—and, I would add, Iraqi police recruits—resistance." About her fellow leftists she writes, "I am not sure how long most of those unconditionally supporting the resistance would have lasted inside Iraq if the militant insurgents responsible for killing and kidnapping Iraqi civilians and foreigners would have . . . prevailed." Of course, those supporters of the resistance never imagined themselves inside Iraq and never thought seriously about the people being killed and kidnapped.

Imagine massive nonviolent Iraqi protests against the occupation. Such protests, Al-Ali writes, would have sent a message that "could not be ignored by Washington and London, *especially if* Iraqis were joined by people from all over the world who took to the streets in solidarity" (my italics). But this solidarity would have had to extend to all the people targeted by the resistance. It would have had to include solidarity against the "increasing attacks on women" by Islamist militants. It would have had to extend to the thousands of Iraqi women—doctors, lawyers, teachers, members of NGOs, politicians, and parliamentarians—who were involved in the attempts to create a new Iraq. Nothing like that emerged.

Al-Ali asks whether "between the American and British occupation and the increasing threat of conservative and extremist forces, the former is the lesser of two evils." I don't think that she was ever ready to give an affirmative answer to that question (as I would). Her opposition to the occupation regime was unrelenting. But she recognized in 2011 that "a considerable number of women activists preferred US and UK troops to remain [in Iraq] until the threat of Islamist militancy, random violent attacks, and sectarian violence has been controlled." I know of very few American leftists who were capable of a similar recognition or who were willing even to consider such a preference—even though it was the preference of women who are certainly our comrades. Whether we American leftists should have supported a delayed withdrawal from Iraq is an open question that I won't try to resolve here; I only want to argue again for the need to listen to comrades abroad—in this case, to Iraqi feminists.

Here is Al-Ali's summary statement on the complex formation of our battles: "We have . . . been hugely inspired and educated by the numerous Iraqi women's rights activists who are fighting on many fronts simultaneously: a foreign military intervention, capitalist expansion, Islamist extremists, and local patriarchal forces. Their struggles and campaigns deserve . . . more widespread acknowledgment and support." Amen.

Many leftists are willing to fight on any one of Al-Ali's four fronts, but to fight on all of them, all at once, has never been a popular version of left politics. We are accustomed to battles in which we join the good guys against the bad guys. Battles in which we have to oppose two sides for the sake of vulnerable men and women who don't yet form a side of their own—this is very difficult. Often, I think, leftism requires that we fight in the name of the unnamed—people like the Iraqi women after 2003 who didn't, and don't yet, have a clear political identity, a party of their own, local or global recognition. And the goal in any such engagement is to encourage those people to speak out, to recognize their agency, to give them names and voices. Fighting on many fronts means acknowledging that we have many enemies. But it also means being faithful to people in trouble, people not willing to be victims, looking to defend themselves, on their way to democracy and equality, who need our help: our comrades abroad.

Al-Ali is unusual in her recognition of political complexities—far beyond those I have described here. She walks, she says, a path that is "often painful and lonely." But whoever said that left politics would be easy?

Can There Be a Decent Left?

Except for chapter 8, all the chapters in this book are extensively revised versions of essays I have published over the last several decades, mostly in *Dissent*. This one is unrevised; it appears here as it appeared in the spring 2002 issue of *Dissent*, with only minor adjustments to match the style in the rest of the book. It led to many arguments, and out of respect for my critics, I have left it as it was when they first read it. But I will say a few words about the article here. It was written in what looked like the immediate aftermath of the Afghan war. My sense of the war's success soon faded, replaced by a view identical with that expressed by Ellen Willis in the very strong essay, "Why I'm Not for Peace," that I discussed in chapter 4. "My frustration," she wrote, "is not that we took action in Afghanistan but that we have not done enough." Mine, too. We (Americans) contributed to the wrecking of Afghan society, Willis argued, but never committed the resources necessary to its reconstruction. Nor did we accept in good time the help that our allies offered, or do anywhere near enough to strengthen the hands of those Afghans who identified themselves as secular democrats, feminists, or trade unionists. Maybe there weren't enough of these people on the ground, but given the war

we fought and our eagerness to move on (because Baghdad beck-
oned), they never had a chance. Willis gives us a good example
of the politics of distinction: she supported the war but savagely
criticized its conduct.

Several of the themes that figure in the chapters above are
foreshadowed here, although I tried in all those chapters to re-
press the anger I felt in the weeks immediately after 9/11. I was
chastised for not naming the people I was criticizing (the indecent
leftists), but at the time everybody knew the names. I had in mind
comments like Noam Chomsky's response to 9/11 in a radio interview soon after. Chomsky offered his listeners a long list of
American crimes and a description of how the United States "extended its resort to force throughout much of the world." And
then he said: "For the first time, the guns have been directed the
other way." He would deny it, of course, but, as Michael Bérubé
has written, "the line suggests precisely what it seems to suggest:
well, it's about time." It seemed to me in 2002, and it seems to
me today, that American leftists need to work toward a better response to American crimes abroad, a stronger connection to our
fellow citizens, and a greater readiness to recognize and oppose
the crimes of others. The conclusion I reached back then is the
same one I reach today: we need to begin again.

Leftist opposition to the war in Afghanistan faded in November
and December of last year, not only because of the success of the
war but also because of the enthusiasm with which so many Af-
ghanis greeted that success. The pictures of women showing their
smiling faces to the world, of men shaving their beards, of girls
in school, of boys playing soccer in shorts: all this was no doubt a
slap in the face to leftist theories of American imperialism, but also
politically disarming. There was (and is) still a lot to worry about:
refugees, hunger, minimal law and order. But it was suddenly clear,
even to many opponents of the war, that the Taliban regime had
been the biggest obstacle to any serious effort to address the looming humanitarian crisis, and it was the American war that removed

the obstacle. It looked (almost) like a war of liberation, a humanitarian intervention.

But the war was primarily neither of these things; it was a preventive war, designed to make it impossible to train terrorists in Afghanistan and to plan and organize attacks like that of September 11. And that war was never really accepted, in wide sections of the left, as either just or necessary. Recall the standard arguments against it: that we should have turned to the United Nations, that we had to prove the guilt of Al Qaeda and the Taliban and then organize international trials, and that the war, if it was fought at all, had to be fought without endangering civilians. The last point was intended to make fighting impossible. I haven't come across any arguments that seriously tried to describe how this (or any) war could be fought without putting civilians at risk, or to ask what degree of risk might be permissible, or to specify the risks that American soldiers should accept in order to reduce the risk of civilian deaths. All these were legitimate issues in Afghanistan, as they were in the Kosovo and Gulf wars. But among last fall's antiwar demonstrators, "Stop the bombing" wasn't a slogan that summarized a coherent view of the bombing—or of the alternatives to it. The truth is that most leftists were not committed to having a coherent view about things like that; they were committed to oppose the war, and they were prepared to oppose it without regard to its causes or character and without any visible concern about preventing future terrorist attacks.

A few left academics have tried to figure out how many civilians actually died in Afghanistan, aiming at as high a figure as possible, on the assumption, apparently, that if the number is greater than the number of people killed in the Towers, the war is unjust. At the moment, most of the numbers are propaganda; there is no reliable accounting. But the claim that the numbers matter in just this way, that the 3,120th death determines the injustice of the war, is in any case wrong. It denies one of the most basic and best understood moral distinctions: between premediated murder and unintended killing. And the denial isn't accidental, as if the people making it just forgot about, or didn't know about, the everyday moral world. The denial is willful: unintended killing by Americans in Afghanistan counts as murder. This can't be true anywhere else, for anybody else.

The radical failure of the left's response to the events of last fall raises a disturbing question: Can there be a decent left in a superpower? Or, more accurately, in the only superpower? Maybe the guilt produced by living in such a country and enjoying its privileges makes it impossible to sustain a decent (intelligent, responsible, morally nuanced) politics. Maybe festering resentment, ingrown anger, and self-hate are the inevitable result of the long years spent in fruitless opposition to the global reach of American power. Certainly, all those emotions were plain to see in the left's reaction to September 11, in the failure to register the horror of the attack or to acknowledge the human pain it caused, in the *schadenfreude* of so many of the first responses, the barely concealed glee that the imperial state had finally gotten what it deserved. Many people on the left recovered their moral balance in the weeks that followed; there is at least the beginning of what should be a long process of self-examination. But many more have still not brought themselves to think about what really happened.

Is there any way of escaping the politics of guilt and resentment on the home ground of a superpower? We might begin to worry about this question by looking at oppositional politics in older imperial states. I can't do that in any sustained way (historians take note), only very sketchily. The Boer War is a good place to begin, because of the fierce opposition it aroused in England—which wasn't marked, despite the cruelty of the war, by the kind of self-hate that we have seen on the American left. Nor were the "little Englanders" hostile to English politics and culture; they managed to take a stand against the empire without alienating themselves from its home country. Indeed, they were more likely to regard England as the home country of liberalism and parliamentary democracy. After all, the values of parliamentarianism (self-government, free speech, the right of opposition) did not support imperial rule. George Orwell's defense of patriotism seems to me an actual description of the feelings of many English liberals and leftists before his time and after (even of the Marxists, some of the best of whom were historians, like E. P. Thompson, who wrote sympathetically, indeed romantically, about the English people). Later on, during the Thatcher years, and particularly during the Falklands War, the tone of the opposition was more bitter, but by then there was no empire, only sour memories.

I think that the French story is similar. For most of the imperial years, French leftists were as proud of their Frenchness as were people on the right—and perhaps with more justification. For wasn't France the birthplace of enlightenment, universal values, and human rights? The Algerian war gave rise to a more familiar self-hatred, most clearly manifest in Jean-Paul Sartre's defense of FLN terrorism (in his preface to Franz Fanon's *Wretched of the Earth*): "To shoot down a European is to kill two birds with one stone, to destroy an oppressor and the man he oppresses at the same time: there remains a dead man and a free man." This suggests that it is actually a good thing to kill Europeans (they were mostly French), but Sartre did not volunteer to go himself and be killed so that one more Algerian would be a free man. His was a generalized, not a personal, self-hatred.

Why shouldn't the American story be like these two, with long years of healthy oppositionist politics and only episodic resentment? Wasn't America a beacon of light to the old world, a city on a hill, an unprecedented experiment in democratic politics? I grew up with the

Americanism of the popular front in the 1930s and '40s; I look back on it now and think that the Communist Party's effort to create a leftist pop culture, in an instant, as the party line turned, was kitschy and manipulative—and also politically very smart. Paul Robeson's "Ballad for Americans," whatever the quality of the music, provides at least a sense of what an unalienated American radicalism might be like. The days after September 11 would not have been a bad time for a popular front. What had happened that made anything like that unthinkable?

The Cold War, imperial adventures in Central America, Vietnam above all, and then the experience of globalization under American leadership: all these, for good reasons and bad, produced a pervasive leftist view of the United States as global bully, rich, privileged, selfish, hedonist, and corrupt beyond remedy. The sense of a civilizing mission, which must have sustained parts of the British and French left in a more fully imperial setting (read John Stuart Mill on British India), never got off the ground here. Foreign aid, the Peace Corps, and nation-building never took on the dimensions of a "mission"; they were mostly sidelines of US foreign policy, underfunded, frequently in the shade of military operations. Certainly, there has been much to criticize in the policies of every US government since World War II (see virtually any back issue of *Dissent*). And yet the leftist critique—most clearly, I think, from the Vietnam years forward (from the time of "Amerika," Vietcong flags, and breathless trips to the North)—has been stupid, overwrought, grossly inaccurate. It is the product of what Philip Roth, in his novel *I Married a Communist*, aptly described as "the combination of embitterment and not thinking." The left has lost its bearings. Why?

I will suggest four reasons, without claiming that this is an exhaustive list. It is nothing more than a rough argument, an attempt to begin a debate.

1. Ideology: the lingering effects of the Marxist theory of imperialism and of the third worldist doctrines of the '60s and '70s. We
may think that we live in a post-ideological age, and maybe most
of us do, but the traces of old ideologies can be found everywhere
in the discourse of the left. Perhaps the most striking consequence
is the inability of leftists to recognize or acknowledge the power of
religion in the modern world. Whenever writers on the left say that
the root cause of terror is global inequality or human poverty, the
assertion is in fact a denial that religious motives really count. Theology, on this view, is just the temporary, colloquial idiom in which
the legitimate rage of oppressed men and women is expressed. A
few brave leftists described the Taliban regime and the Al Qaeda
movement as examples of "clerical fascism," which at least gets the
adjective right. And maybe "fascist" is close enough, even if this
new politics doesn't look like the product of late capitalist degener-
ation. It gives the left a reason for opposing Islamic terror, which is
an important achievement. But it would be better to find a reason
in the realities of terrorism itself, in the idea of a holy war against
the infidels, which is not the same thing as a war against inferior
races or alien nations. In fact, Islamic radicalism is not, as fascism
is, a racist or ultra-nationalist doctrine. Something else is going on,
which we need to understand.

But ideologically primed leftists were likely to think that they
already understood whatever needed to be understood. Any group
that attacks the imperial power must be a representative of the oppressed, and its agenda must be the agenda of the left. It isn't necessary to listen to its spokesmen. What else can they want except
. . . the redistribution of resources across the globe, the withdrawal
of American soldiers from wherever they are, the closing down of
aid programs for repressive governments, the end of the blockade
of Iraq, and the establishment of a Palestinian state alongside Israel? I don't doubt that there is some overlap between this program

and the dreams of the Al Qaeda leaders—though Al Qaeda is not an egalitarian movement, and the idea that it supports a two-state solution to the Israeli-Palestinian conflict is crazy. The overlap is circumstantial and convenient, nothing more. A holy war against infidels is not, even unintentionally, unconsciously, or "objectively," a left politics. But how many leftists can even imagine a holy war against infidels?

2. Powerlessness and alienation: leftists have no power in the United States and most of us don't expect to exercise power, ever. Many left intellectuals live in America like internal aliens, refusing to identify with their fellow citizens, regarding any hint of patriotic feeling as politically incorrect. That's why they had such difficulty responding emotionally to the attacks of September 11 or joining in the expressions of solidarity that followed. Equally important, that's why their participation in the policy debate after the attacks was so odd; their proposals (turn to the United Nations, collect evidence against bin Laden, and so on) seem to have been developed with no concern for effectiveness and no sense of urgency. They talked and wrote as if they could not imagine themselves responsible for the lives of their fellow citizens. That was someone else's business; the business of the left was . . . what? To oppose the authorities, whatever they did. The good result of this opposition was a spirited defense of civil liberties. But even this defense displayed a certain willful irresponsibility and ineffectiveness because so many leftists rushed to the defense of civil liberties while refusing to acknowledge that the country faced real dangers—as if there was no need at all to balance security and freedom. Maybe the right balance will emerge spontaneously from the clash of right-wing authoritarianism and left-wing absolutism, but it would be better practice for the left to figure out the right balance for itself, on its own; the effort would suggest a responsible politics and a real desire to exercise power some day.

But what really marks the left, or a large part of it, is the bitterness that comes with abandoning any such desire. The alienation is radical. How else can one understand the unwillingness of people who, after all, live here, and whose children and grandchildren live here, to join in a serious debate about how to protect the country against future terrorist attacks? There is a pathology in this unwillingness, and it has already done us great damage.

3. The moral purism of blaming America first: many leftists seem to believe that this is like blaming oneself, taking responsibility for the crimes of the imperial state. In fact, when we blame America, we also lift ourselves above the blameworthy (other) Americans. The left sets itself apart. Whatever America is doing in the world *isn't* our doing. In some sense, of course, that is true. The defeat of fascism in the middle years of the twentieth century and of communism in the last years were not our doing. Some of us, at least, thought that these efforts merited our support—or our "critical support." But this is a complicated and difficult politics, and it doesn't allow for the favorite posture of many American leftists: standing as a righteous minority, brave and determined, among the timid, the corrupt, and the wicked. A posture like that ensures at once the moral superiority of the left and its political failure.

4. The sense of not being entitled to criticize anyone else: how can we live here in America, the richest, most powerful, and most privileged country in the world, and say anything critical about people who are poorer and weaker than we are? This was a major issue in the 1960s, when the New Left seemed to have discovered "oppression" for the first time, and we all enlisted on the side of oppressed men and women and failed, again and again, to criticize the authoritarianism and brutality that often scars their politics. There is no deeper impulse in left politics than this enlistment; solidarity with people in trouble seems to me the most profound commitment that leftists make. But this solidarity includes, or should

include, a readiness to tell these people when we think they are acting wrongly, violating the values we share. Even the oppressed have obligations, and surely the first among these is not to murder innocent people, not to make terrorism their politics. Leftists who cannot insist upon this point, even to people poorer and weaker than themselves, have abandoned both politics and morality for something else. They are radical only in their abjection. That was Sartre's radicalism, face to face with FLN terror, and it has been imitated by thousands since, excusing and apologizing for acts that any decent left would begin by condemning.

What ought to be done? I have a modest agenda: *put decency first*, and then we will see. So, let's go back over my list of reasons for the current indecency.

Ideology. We certainly need something better than the ragtag Marxism with which so much of the left operates today—whose chief effect is to turn world politics into a cheap melodrama, with all the villains dressed to look the part and with one villain larger than life. A tough materialist analysis would be fine, so long as it is sophisticated enough to acknowledge that material interests don't exhaust the possibilities of human motivation. The spectacle of European leftists straining to find some economic reason for the Kosovo war (oil in the Balkans? a possible pipeline? was NATO reaching for control of the Black Sea?) was entertaining at the time, but it doesn't bear repeating. For the moment we can make do with a little humility, an openness to heterodox ideas, a sharp eye for the real world, and a readiness to attend to moral as well as materialist arguments. This last point is especially important. The encounter with Islamic radicalism, and with other versions of politicized religion, should help us understand that high among our interests are our values: secular enlightenment, human rights, and democratic government. Left politics starts with the defense of these three.

Alienation and powerlessness. It is a common idea on the left that political responsibility is something like temperance, moderation, and cleanliness—they are all good bourgeois values that are incompatible with radical politics or incisive social criticism. You have to be a little wild to be a radical. That isn't a crazy idea, and alienated intellectuals may well have, more than anyone else, the anger necessary to begin the critical project and the lust for intellectual combat that sustains it. But they don't necessarily get things right, and the angrier they are and the more they are locked into their combative posture, the more likely they are to get things wrong. What was necessary after September 11, and what is necessary now, is an engagement with our fellow citizens that recognizes the fellowship. We can be as critical as we like, but these are people whose fate we share; we are responsible for their safety as they are for ours, and our politics has to reflect that mutual responsibility. When they are attacked, so are we; and we should join willingly and constructively in debates about how to defend our country. Once again: we should act as if we won't always be powerless.

Blaming America first. Not everything that goes badly in the world goes badly because of us. The United States is not omnipotent, and its leaders should not be taken as co-conspirators in every human disaster. The left has little difficulty understanding the need for distributive justice with regard to resources, but we have been practically clueless about the just distribution of praise and blame. To take the obvious example: in the second half of the twentieth century, the United States fought both just and unjust wars, undertook both just and unjust interventions. It would be a useful exercise to work through the lists and test our capacity to make distinctions—to recognize, say, that the United States was wrong in Guatemala in 1956 and right in Kosovo in 1999. Why can't we accept an ambivalent relation to American power, acknowledging that it has had good and bad effects in the world? But shouldn't an internationalist left demand a more egalitarian distribution of power? Well, yes, in principle; but any actual redistribution will have to be judged by the quality of the states that would be empowered by it. Faced with states like, say, Saddam Hussein's Iraq, I don't think we have to support a global redistribution of political power.

Not blaming anyone else. The world (and this includes the third world) is too full of hatred, cruelty, and corruption for any left, even the American left, to suspend its judgment about what's going on. It's not the case that because we are privileged, we should turn inward and focus our criticism only on ourselves. In fact, inwardness is one of our privileges; it is often a form of political self-indulgence. Yes, we are entitled to blame the others whenever they are blameworthy; in fact, it is only when we do that, when we denounce, say, the authoritarianism of third world governments, that we will find our true comrades—the local opponents of the Maximal Leaders and military juntas, who are often waiting for our recognition and support. If we value democracy, we have to be prepared to defend it, at home, of course, but not only there.

I would once have said that we were well along: the American left has an honorable history, and we have certainly gotten some things right, above all, our opposition to domestic and global inequalities. But what the aftermath of September 11 suggests is that we have not advanced very far—and not always in the right direction. The left needs to begin again.

Notes

Introduction

1. Robert A. Rosenstone, *Romantic Revolutionary: A Biography of John Reed* (New York: Vintage, 1981), 276.
2. Edward Abrahams, *The Lyrical Left: Randolph Bourne and Alfred Stiglitz and the Origins of Cultural Radicalism in America* (Charlottesville: University Press of Virginia, 1988), 89, quoting Floyd Dell.
3. Randolph Bourne, "The War and the Intellectuals" and "A War Diary," in *The World of Randolph Bourne: An Anthology of Essays and Letters*, ed. Lillian Schlissel (New York: Dutton, 1965), 154, 189.
4. Andrew Bacevich, "Cultivating Our Own Garden," in *In Search of Progressive America*, ed. Michael Kazin (Philadelphia: University of Pennsylvania Press, 2008), 36.
5. Andrew Bacevich, *American Empire: The Realities and Consequences of U.S. Diplomacy* (Cambridge: Harvard University Press, 2004), 12–20; Charles A. Beard, *A Foreign Policy for America* (New York: Knopf, 1940).
6. William L. O'Neill, *A Better World: The Great Schism; Stalinism and the American Intellectuals* (New York: Simon and Schuster, 1982), 33.
7. Jeff Faux responding to my *Dissent* article "A Foreign Policy for the Left" (Spring 2014), the immediate precursor to this book; posted on the *Dissent* website under the title "Defending the 'Default Position,'" https://www.dissentmagazine.org/author/eric-alterman-jeff-faux-and-michael-walzer.

8. Richard Rorty, *Achieving Our Country: Leftist Thought in Twentieth-Century America* (Cambridge: Harvard University Press, 1999).

9. Václav Havel, *NATO, Europe, and the Security of Democracy: Speeches, Articles, and Interviews, 1990–2002* (Pardubice, Czech Republic: Theo Publishing, 2002), 38.

ONE

Moments in Time

1. Michael Bérubé, *Rhetorical Occasions: Essays on Humans and the Humanities* (Chapel Hill: University of North Carolina Press, 2006), 241; references to Rorty's *Achieving Our Country* can be found there.

2. Jane Bennett, "From the Editor," *Political Theory* 14 (February 2016), 3.

3. George C. Herring, *From Colony to Superpower: U.S. Foreign Relations since 1776* (New York: Oxford University Press, 2008), 156.

4. All the issues of the *Democratic Review* can be found online at http://ebooks .library.cornell.edu/u/usde/usde.html. The quotes here are from the June 1852 issue.

5. Robert A. Rosenstone, *Romantic Revolutionary: A Biography of John Reed* (New York: Vintage, 1981), 378.

6. Isaac Deutscher, *The Prophet Armed: Trotsky, 1879–1921* (New York: Oxford University Press, 1954), 463ff.

7. Irving Howe, *A Margin of Hope: An Intellectual Autobiography* (San Diego: Harcourt Brace Jovanovich, 1982), 105.

8. George Lichtheim, *Europe and America: The Future of the Atlantic Community* (London: Thames and Hudson, 1963), 43–57; Nicolaus Mills, *Winning the Peace: The Marshall Plan and America's Coming of Age as a Superpower* (Hoboken: John Wiley and Sons, 2008), especially chapters 9, 10.

9. *Must We Arm? Hillquit-Gardner Debate* (New York: Rand School of Social Science, 1916), 29.

10. See my *Dissent* pamphlet *Cuba: The Invasion and the Consequences* (June 1961), 12. It was Theodore Draper who unearthed this quote from an interview Castro gave to an Italian magazine: see Draper, "Castro's Cuba," *New Leader*, March 1961.

11. C. Wright Mills, *Listen, Yankee: The Revolution in Cuba* (New York: Ballantine Books, 1960), 182.

12. Edward Friedman and Richard Kraus, "The Two Sides of Castro's Cuba," *Dissent* (Winter 1961), 58.

13. Leszek Kolakowski, "The Heritage of the Left," in *Is God Happy? Selected Essays* (New York: Basic Books, 2013), 45.

14. Harold Brackman, *Jews, African Americans, and Israel: The Ties That Bind* (Los

Angeles: Simon Wiesenthal Center/Museum of Tolerance, January–February 2010).

15. Frantz Fanon, *The Wretched of the Earth*, trans. Constance Farrington (New York: Grove, 1963), 18–19 (Sartre's preface); Michael Walzer, *Just and Unjust Wars* (New York: Basic Books, 1977), 204–205.

16. "Bring the Boys Home," lyrics by Freda Payne, Invictus Records, #9092.

17. Kevin Mattson, *Intellectuals in Action: The Origins of the New Left and Radical Liberalism, 1945–1970* (University Park: Pennsylvania State University Press, 2002), 157.

18. Fred H. Harrington, "The Anti-Imperialist Movement in the United States, 1898–1900," *Mississippi Valley Historical Review* 22 (September 1935), 211–230.

19. Mark Twain, *To the Person Sitting in Darkness*, in *Mark Twain's Weapons of Satire: Anti-Imperialist Writings on the Philippine-American War*, ed. Jim Zwick (New York: Syracuse University Press, 1992). "Comments on the Moro Massacre," March 12, 1906, can be found in the same volume, 170–173.

20. Claire Hirshfield, "The Anglo-Boer War and the Issue of Jewish Culpability," *Journal of Contemporary History*, Sage 15 (1980), 619–631 (quote on 623).

21. For a persuasive and engaging account of the anti-war struggle, see Michael Kazin, *War against War: The American Fight for Peace, 1914–1918* (New York: Simon and Schuster, 1917).

22. *Must We Arm?*, 39.

23. Michael Bérubé, *The Left at War* (New York: New York University Press, 2009), 131.

24. For the British left in the 1930s, I have relied on Martin Gilbert, *The Roots of Appeasement* (New York: New American Library, 1966); and Keith Robbins, *Munich 1938* (London: Cassell, 1968). The Atlee quote is from Gilbert, *The Roots of Appeasement*, 186.

25. Max Lerner, *Ideas for the Ice Age: Studies in a Revolutionary Era* (1941; Westport, CT: Greenwood Press, 1974; originally published 1941), 350.

26. Norman Thomas and Bertram D. Wolfe, *Keep America Out of War: A Program* (New York: Frederick A. Stokes, 1939).

27. Howe, *A Margin of Hope*, 87.

28. Paul Berman, *Terror and Liberalism* (New York: Norton, 2004), 126.

29. Dwight Macdonald, *Memoirs of a Revolutionist: Essays in Political Criticism* (New York: Farrar, Straus and Cudahy, 1957). For "Looking at the War" see pp. 107–201.

30. Michael Harrington, *Fragments of a Century: A Social Autobiography* (New York: E. P. Dutton, 1973), 68–69; I. F. Stone, *The Hidden History of the Korean War, 1950–1951* (New York: Monthly Review Press, 1952).

31. Willis's work is extensively discussed in Bérubé, *The Left at War*; for her views on the Afghan war, see 156–157. See also below, chapter 4.

32. Michael Kazin, *American Dreamers: How the Left Changed a Nation* (New York: Knopf, 2011), 233.
33. *The Black Book of Bosnia: The Consequences of Appeasement*, ed. Nader Mousavizadeh (New York: New Republic Books, 1996); Samantha Powers, *A Problem from Hell: America and the Age of Genocide* (New York: Basic Books, 2002).
34. Bérubé, *The Left at War*, 148.
35. Albert Fried, ed., *Socialism in America: A Documentary History* (Garden City, NY: Anchor, 1970), 523.
36. Patrick Wintour, "Miliband: UK Has Moral Duty to Intervene," *The Guardian*, February 11, 2008.
37. Stephen J. Whitfield, *A Critical American: The Politics of Dwight Macdonald* (Hamden, CT: Archon, 1984), 126.
38. See Ignacio Walker, "The Three Lefts of Latin America," *Dissent* (Fall 2008), https://www.dissentmagazine.org/article/the-three-lefts-of-latin-america. Walker's three are the Marxist, populist, and social-democratic lefts.

TWO

What Is Left Internationalism?

1. Stuart Hall, "The Toad in the Garden: Thatcherism among the Theorists," in *Marxism and the Interpretation of Culture*, ed. Cary Nelson and Lawrence Grossman (Urbana: University of Illinois Press, 1988), 44. See discussion in Michael Bérubé, *The Left at War* (New York: New York University Press, 2009), 163–167.
2. Ignazio Silone, "The Choice of Comrades," trans. Darina Silone, in *Voices of Dissent* (New York: Grove, 1958), 328.
3. Norman Geras, *The Contract of Mutual Indifference: Political Philosophy after the Holocaust* (London: Verso, 1998), 75.
4. Ibid.
5. Leon Trotsky, *Bulletin of the Opposition*, no. 41 (January 1935).
6. George Orwell, *The Road to Wigan Pier* (New York: Harcourt, Brace, 1958), 180.
7. Bertolt Brecht, *Selected Poems*, trans. H. R. Hays (New York: Grove, 1947), 176 ("To Posterity").
8. *Hayim Greenberg Anthology*, ed. Marie Syrkin (Detroit: Wayne State University Press, 1968), 291.
9. Geras, *The Contract of Mutual Indifference*, 59.
10. Tony Judt, *Postwar: A History of Europe since 1945* (New York: Penguin, 2005), 574. See "Anatomy of a Reticence" in Václav Havel, *Open Letters: Selected Writings, 1965–1990* (New York: Vintage, 1992), 291–322.
11. Danny Postel, *Reading Legitimation Crisis in Tehran: Iran and the Future of Liberalism* (Chicago: Prickly Paradigm Press, 2006), 14.

12. Leszek Kolakowski, "My Correct Views about Everything," in *Is God Happy? Selected Essays* (New York: Basic Books, 2013), 127; Postel, *Reading Legitimation Crisis in Tehran*, 14–15.
13. Postel, *Reading Legitimation Crisis in Tehran*, 50.
14. Ibid.
15. Ibid., 13.

THREE
In Defense of Humanitarian Intervention

1. See, for example, W. E. Hall, *International Law*, 5th ed. (Oxford: Oxford University Press, 1904), 289ff.
2. Michael Zantovsky, *Havel* (London: Atlantic Books, 2014), 435.
3. For all the arguments in the debate, see William Joseph Buckley, ed., *Kosovo: Contending Voices on Balkan Interventions* (Grand Rapids, MI: Eerdmans, 2000).
4. See the useful essays in James M. Radcliffe, *The Good Samaritan and the Law* (Garden City, NY: Anchor Books, Doubleday, 1966).
5. Cf. Daniel Statman, "Who Needs Imperfect Duties?" in *American Philosophical Quarterly* 33 (April 1996), 211–224.
6. Jean-Jacques Rousseau, *The Social Contract*, Bk. II, ch. 3.
7. This is the argument of David Rieff, *Slaughterhouse: Bosnia and the Failure of the West* (New York: Touchstone, Simon and Schuster, 1996).
8. Michael Walzer, *Just and Unjust Wars* (New York: Basic Books, 1977), chapter 6.
9. Michael W. Doyle, *UN Peacekeeping in Cambodia: UNTAC's Civil Mandate* (Boulder, CO: Lynne Rienner, 1995).
10. Michael Walzer, "The Politics of Rescue," *Dissent* (Winter 1995), 35–40.
11. On the possible role of the United Nations, see Michael Doyle, "The New Interventionism," *Metaphilosophy* 32 (January 2001), 212–235.
12. For a strong argument along these lines, see Aryeh Neier, *War Crimes: Brutality, Genocide, Terror, and the Struggle for Justice* (New York: New York Times Books, Random House, 1998).
13. J. S. Mill, "A Few Words on Non-Intervention," in *Dissertations and Discussions* (New York: H. Holt, 1873), III, 238–263.
14. Killian Clarke, "The Politics of Refugee Relief," *Dissent* (Summer 2016), 100; see also Muhammad Idrees Ahmad, "What Do Syrians Want?" in the same issue, which I draw on in the following paragraph.
15. Edward Luttwak, "No-Score War," *Times Literary Supplement*, July 14, 2000, 11, reviewing Michael Ignatieff, *Virtual War: Kosovo and Beyond* (New York: Picador, 2000).

FOUR
Is There an American Empire?

1. Michael Hardt and Antonio Negri, *Empire* (Cambridge: Harvard University Press, 2000), 344–345.

2. John Bellamy Foster, "Imperial America and War," *Monthly Review* 55 (May 2003), https://monthlyreview.org/2003/05/01/imperial-america-and-war/. But Foster himself is seriously engaged with politics.

3. Michael Ignatieff, *Empire Lite: Nation-Building in Bosnia, Kosovo, Afghanistan* (New York: Vintage, 2004).

4. Chantal Mouffe, ed., *Gramsci and Marxist Theory* (London: Routledge and Kegan Paul, 1979), 86–87.

5. Stuart Hall, "Gramsci's Relevance for the Study of Race and Ethnicity," in *Stuart Hall: Critical Dialogues in Cultural Studies*, ed. David Morley and Kuan-Hsing Chen (New York: Routledge, 1996), 424. See the admiring discussion of Hall's politics in Michael Bérubé, *The Left at War* (New York: New York University Press, 2009), 160–207.

6. Bérubé, *The Left at War,* 172.

7. Ellen Willis, "Why I'm Not for Peace," *Radical Society*, April 2002, 14–15. See Bérubé, *The Left at War,* 156–159.

8. Theodore Roosevelt, "Roosevelt Corollary to the Monroe Doctrine," December 6, 1904, *Teaching American History*, http://teachingamericanhistory.org/library/document/roosevelt-corollary-to-monroe-doctrine/.

9. See, for example, Dan Kovalik, "Russia and the New Cold War in Historical Context: Part II of Conversations with Russian Scholar Stephen Cohen," *Huffington Post*, July 13, 2016 (updated), http://www.huffingtonpost.com/dan-kovalik/russia—the-new-cold-war_b_7784832.html.

10. Karl Marx, *Early Writings*, ed. T. B. Bottomore (London: C. A. Watts, 1963), 193–194.

11. V. I. Lenin, *What the "Friends of the People" Are* (Moscow: Progress Publishers, 1951), 286.

12. Michael Rustin, *For a Pluralist Socialism* (London: Verso, 1985), 249, 252.

13. Hardt and Negri, *Empire,* 36.

14. Martin Walker, "America's Virtual Empire," *World Policy Journal* 19 (Summer 2002), 13–20.

FIVE
Global and Domestic Justice

1. Jean-Jacques Rousseau, "A Discourse on the Origin of Inequality," in *The Social Contract and Discourses*, trans. G. D. H. Cole (New York: E. P. Dutton,

1950), 226; John Rawls, *A Theory of Justice* (Cambridge: Belknap/Harvard University Press, 1971), 338–339.

2. David Miller, "Distributing Responsibilities," *Journal of Political Philosophy* 9:4 (December 2001), 453–471.

3. Thomas Pogge, *World Poverty and Human Rights* (Cambridge, UK: Polity Press, 2002), 204–205.

4. Paul Collier, "Why the Poorest Countries Are Failing and What Can Be Done About It," in *WIDER Angle*, no. 2 (Helsinki: World Institute for Development Economics Research, 2007), 2. See also Collier, *The Bottom Billion* (Oxford: Oxford University Press, 2007).

5. My argument here is meant to be consistent with my argument in *Spheres of Justice: A Defense of Pluralism and Equality* (New York: Basic Books, 1983)—a book in which I fell into the default position, arguing only about justice at home.

SIX

World Government and the Politics of Pretending

1. Immanuel Kant, "Eternal Peace," in *The Philosophy of Kant*, ed. Carl J. Friedrich (New York: Modern Library, 1949), 454.

2. Jack Jacobs, *On Socialists and "The Jewish Question" after Marx* (New York: New York University Press, 1992), 80. There were more sympathetic views, at least of "revolutionary nationalism." See John Schwarzmantel, *Socialism and the Idea of the Nation* (New York: Harvester Wheatsheaf, 1991).

3. But the Kurds, especially the Syrian Kurds, have found some support on the left: see Meredith Tax, *A Road Unforeseen: Women Fight the Islamic State* (New York: Bellevue Literary Press, 2016).

4. To get a sense of the fury, visit the website of the BDS (Boycott, Divestment, and Sanctions) Movement. For a left Zionist response, see Cary Nelson, ed., *Dreams Deferred: A Concise Guide to the Israeli-Palestinian Conflict and the Movement to Boycott Israel* (Bloomington: Indiana University Press, 2016).

5. The phrase is attributed to the German social-democrat August Bebel; it was in general use among social-democrats in the 1890s. Richard J. Evans, *The Coming of the Third Reich* (New York: Penguin, 2005), 496.

6. John Locke, *"The Second Treatise of Civil Government" and "A Letter Concerning Toleration,"* ed. J. W. Gough (Oxford: Basil Blackwell, 1948), 156–157.

7. Ibid., 158.

8. See Robert Frost's "Mending Wall," first published in 1914. In this poem about a New England village, Frost's argument is different from mine, but my paraphrase is right for international society.

9. Michael Rustin, *For a Pluralist Socialism* (London: Verso, 1985), 256–257.

10. Jonathan Schell, *The Fate of the Earth* (New York: Knopf, 1982), 218; Anthony Barnett, *Iron Britannia* (London: Allison and Busby, 1982), 148.

11. See the account and strong critique in Samantha Powers, *A Problem from Hell: America and the Age of Genocide* (New York: Basic Books, 2002), chapter 10.

12. Gwen P. Barnes, "The International Criminal Court's Ineffective Enforcement Mechanisms: The Indictment of President Omar Al-Bashir," *Fordham International Law Journal* 34:6 (2011), 1583–1616.

SEVEN

The Left and Religion

1. Nick Cohen, *What's Left: How Liberals Lost Their Way* (London: Fourth Estate, 2007), 361.

2. Deepa Kumar, *Islamophobia and the Politics of Empire* (Chicago: Haymarket Books, 2012).

3. David J. Rusin, "Islamists Inflate the Number of Anti-Muslim Crimes in Order to Silence Critics," *National Review*, January 11, 2013.

4. "Attacks against Muslim Americans Fueled Rise in Hate Crimes, F.B.I. Says," *New York Times*, November 16, 2016, A13.

5. Geert Wilders: open letter to the Dutch newspaper *Die Volkskrant*, August 8, 2007; Hans-Jürgen Irmer: speech in the Hesse state parliament, March 5, 2014.

6. Pascal Bruckner, *The Tyranny of Guilt: An Essay on Western Masochism*, trans. Steven Rendall (Princeton, NJ: Princeton University Press, 2010), 48.

7. Paul Berman and Michael Walzer, "Que révèle la polémique Kamel Daoud?," *Le Monde*, March 30, 2016, 22.

8. Edward W. Said, *Orientalism* (New York: Vintage, 1979), 332, 318.

9. Edward W. Said, *The Question of Palestine* (New York: Vintage, 1980), 184.

10. Hatem Bazian and Maxwell Leung, Editorial Statement, *Islamophobia Studies Journal* (Spring 2014), http://crg.berkeley.edu/content/isj-spring2014.

11. Hatem Bazian, "Deconstructing Islamophobia in Muslim Majority States," *Daily Sabah*, July 28, 2014, http://www.dailysabah.com/opinion/2014/07/28/deconstructing-islamophobia-in-muslim-majority-states.

12. Nikolas Kozloff, "A Tale of Boko Haram, Political Correctness, Feminism, and the Left," *Huffington Post*, July 30, 2014 (updated), http://www.huffingtonpost.com/nikolas-kozloff/a-tale-of-boko-haram-poli_b_5421960.html.

13. David Swanson, "What to Do about ISIS," *War Is a Crime.org*, August 28, 2014, http://warisacrime.org/content/what-do-about-isis; Swanson, "What to Do about ISIS," *Tikkun Daily*, September 3, 2014, http://www.tikkun.org/tikkundaily/2014/09/03/what-to-do-about-isis/.

14. Leo Igwe, "Is the Boko Haram Menace Rooted in Poverty or Fanaticism?" *Left Foot Forward*, May 12, 2014, https://leftfootforward.org/2014/05/is-the -boko-haram-menace-rooted-in-poverty-or-fanaticism/.

15. Parvez Ahmed, "Boko Haram and Bill Maher Are Both Wrong," *Huffington Post*, July 19, 2014 (updated), http://www.huffingtonpost.com/parvez-ahmed/boko -haram-and-bill-maher_b_5334872.html.

16. Fawaz A. Gerges, *Journey of the Jihadist: Inside Muslim Militancy* (Orlando, FL: Harcourt, 2006).

17. Susan Watkins, "Editorial," *New Left Review* 28 (July 1, 2004), 1–13.

18. Fred Halliday, "The Jihadism of Fools," *Dissent* (Winter 2007), 53–56.

19. Slavoj Žižek, *Violence* (New York: Picador, 2008), 187, 139.

20. "Judith Butler on Hamas, Hezbollah & the Israeli Lobby (2006)," *Radical Archives*, March 28, 2010, https://radicalarchives.org/2010/03/28/jbut ler-on-hamas-hezbollah-israel-lobby/; "Judith Butler Responds to Attack: 'I Affirm a Judaism That Is Not Associated with State Violence,'" *Mondoweiss*, August 27, 2012, http://mondoweiss.net/2012/08/judith-butler-responds-to -attack-i-affirm-a-judaism-that-is-not-associated-with-state-violence/.

21. Janet Afary and Kevin B. Anderson, *Foucault and the Iranian Revolution: Gender and the Seductions of Islamism* (Chicago: University of Chicago Press, 2005), 125.

22. Emmanuel Sivan, *Radical Islam: Medieval Theology and Modern Politics* (New Haven: Yale University Press, 1985), 158.

23. Robert Birnbaum, "Azar Nafisi," Author Interview, *Identity Theory*, February 5, 2004, http://www.identitytheory.com/?s=azar+nafisi&searchsubmit=Find. I thank Nick Cohen for this reference.

24. Anne Norton, *On the Muslim Question* (Princeton, NJ: Princeton University Press, 2013). To be fair, Norton was writing before the appearance of the ISIS Caliphate.

25. Dan Diner, *Lost in the Sacred: Why the Muslim World Stood Still*, trans. Steven Rendall (Princeton, NJ: Princeton University Press, 2009), 3.

26. Michael Hardt and Antonio Negri, *Empire* (Cambridge: Harvard University Press, 2000), 149.

27. Paul Berman, *The Flight of the Intellectuals: The Controversy over Islamism and the Press* (Brooklyn: Melville House, 2011), chapters 8–9; Katha Pollitt, "David Horowitz, Feminist?," *The Nation*, November 1, 2007, https://www .thenation.com/article/david-horowitz-feminist/.

28. Meredith Tax, *Double Bind: The Muslim Right, the Anglo-American Left, and Universal Human Rights* (New York: Center for Secular Space, 2012), 82. For more information about WLUML, see Madhavi Sunder, "Piercing the Veil," *Yale Law Journal* 112 (April 2003), 1434–1443.

EIGHT

The Complex Formation of Our Battles

1. Irving Howe, *A Margin of Hope: An Intellectual Autobiography* (San Diego: Harcourt Brace Jovanovich, 1982), 132.
2. William Butler Yeats, "The Great Day" (1913).
3. Hayim Greenberg, "Socialism Re-examined," in *Hayim Greenberg Anthology*, ed. Marie Syrkin (Detroit, MI: Wayne State University Press, 1968), 201.
4. For a partial account and some of the numbers, see Robert Conquest, *The Great Terror: Stalin's Purge of the Thirties* (London: Macmillan, 1968).
5. A useful example: Sophie Wahnich, *In Defense of the Terror: Liberty and Death in the French Revolution*, trans. David Fernbach (London: Verso, 2012).
6. Alan Johnson, "Slavoj Žižek's Theory of Revolution: A Critique," *Global Discourse* 2:1 (2011), 135–151.
7. Adam Kirsch, "The Deadly Jester," *New Republic*, December 2, 2008, https://newrepublic.com/article/60979/the-deadly-jester.
8. See Paul Bowman and Richard Stamp, eds., *The Truth of Žižek* (London: Continuum, 2007).
9. Kanan Makiya, *The Rope* (New York: Pantheon, 2016), 207 ("A Personal Note").
10. Nadje Al-Ali, "A Feminist Perspective on the Iraq War," *Works and Days* 57/58, 29 (Spring/Fall 2011). Quotations that follow are from pp. 12–13.

Index

Index